WE COMMAND ALL NATIONS TO KEEP THE PEACE.

Dr. J. H. McLean's
PEACE-MAKERS.

"This work is more than opportune—it is imperative."—VICTOR HUGO.

Dr. JAMES HENRY McLEAN, OF St. LOUIS, Mo.
PROJECTOR, INVENTOR AND PATENTEE,

WITH

MYRON COLONEY, OF NEW HAVEN, CONN.
MECHANICAL INVENTOR AND PATENTEE.

The Naval & Military Press Ltd

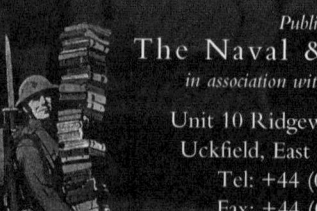

UKASE.

WE COMMAND ALL NATIONS TO KEEP THE PEACE.

Dr. J. H. McLEAN'S
PEACE-MAKERS.

"This work is more than opportune—it is imperative."—VICTOR HUGO.

Dr. JAMES HENRY McLEAN, OF ST. LOUIS, MO.
PROJECTOR, INVENTOR AND PATENTEE,

WITH

MYRON COLONEY, OF NEW HAVEN, CONN.
MECHANICAL INVENTOR AND PATENTEE.

Entered according to Act of Congress, in the year eighteen hundred and eighty, by
Dr. JAMES HENRY McLEAN,
In the Office of the Librarian of Congress, at Washington.

Dedication.

TO JAMES GORDON BENNETT.

Being profoundly impressed with the idea that the human race is now crossing the threshold of a new epoch of expert industry and enlightened commercial and social intercourse, and that the maintenance of an unbroken and universal peace is an indispensable condition to its success, mature reflection has convinced me that my life can not be more nobly devoted than in creating conditions which shall insure such peace.

In view of the defects of human nature and the mad ambitions of personal rulers, it is evident that universal peace can be maintained only by making war so terrible and devastating as to shock every community and cause them to rise *en masse* and declare that the slaughter of their fellows must cease! that for the gratification of no man's morbid ambition, for the acquisition of no territory, for the alteration of no boundary, for the enlargement of no domain, or for the righting of no fancied wrong, will they ever invade any other nation's territory; and only to repel invasion and to maintain local peace will they ever consent to be marshaled with deadly weapons in their hands.

This volume illustrates and describes the unwearied and expensive efforts I have already made in this direction. It is my intention to continue these efforts in the future.

This vast work which I have undertaken, is merely a continuation of my professional labors, under the inspiration of the motto, "SAVE THE LIVES OF THE PEOPLE," which still persistently urges me on.

It seems eminently fitting that I should dedicate this volume to the head of the grandest and most independent newspaper on earth, the unrivaled educator of the people; to one who, while daily accomplishing unparalleled feats of journalism, finds time to restore eminent travelers to their friends, to rectify the geography of a vast continent, to penetrate the mysteries of the Polar Circle, and to rescue nearly four millions of destitute people in Ireland from starvation. America thrills with commendable pride when the name of James Gordon Bennett is mentioned—the leading journalist of the world. Permit me, therefore, to acknowledge my appreciation of your inestimable services to mankind by dedicating this volume to you and calling my chief shoulder gun by your name, "The James Gordon Bennett Rifle."

DR. JAMES HENRY McLEAN.

ST. LOUIS, MO., JULY, 1880.

INTRODUCTION.

It is impossible for human beings to attain to their highest development on earth, so long as they are exposed to the unrestrained passions and depredations of large bodies of armed men. Nothing on earth is of as much consequence *as human beings*, and nothing so much concerns them as their own individual peace and comfort while upon the earth. Therefore, governments were instituted, that, by means of effective co-operative effort, depredators, freebooters, pirates, brigands, and common robbers and highwaymen, should be overawed, and the peaceful and industriously inclined classes should be assured of safety and comfort in the pursuit of their industries. The power to wield the armed forces of a government had necessarily to be intrusted to a few, and in process of time these few, favored by the impregnability of their positions, assumed the right to become permanent dictators, and the masses were compelled to accept such assumption as Divinely imposed, because they had no means of successfully resisting it. Upon such a foundation is based the pretension of all those who belong to what they choose to denominate the "governing classes," and the trivial disputes, small jealousies, unworthy ambitions or censurable covetousness of these same self styled "governing classes," have strewn the earth with slain, and drenched her fair fields with blood, for many thousand years.

It is time, therefore, that the nations be commanded to keep the peace; that the prevailing epoch of scientific industry may have full and undisturbed course among all peoples; and that human beings, individually and collectively, be guaranteed immunity from assault and forcible seizure of person and effects, either as the result of inimical invasion or forced service in the armies of a government.

Under existing circumstances universal peace can be secured only by making warfare so extremely dreadful that the entire world will be appalled at the result of every battle. In ancient times, when men depended upon the sling, arrow, spear, lance and sword to destroy each other's lives, battles lasting for several days were frequently fought with no very sanguinary result, unless one army became panic-stricken and turned its back upon its opponent, then, indeed, the slaughter has been sometimes dreadfully severe, but usually the loss has been light; and with a few hundred thousand men, bold leaders, like Alexander, Pompey, Xerxes, and Julius Cæsar, subdued entire continents. When firearms supplanted the more primitive weapons, the loss of life in engagements was heavily increased, and the duration of battles greatly shortened. As improvements have been made in these agents of destruction, from time to time, the percentage of lives destroyed within a given time in battle has been very greatly augmented. Dr. JAMES HENRY MCLEAN, of St. Louis, Mo., conceived the idea, that important improvements could be made, amounting to an entire revolution, in life destroying mechanisms, under the conviction that this only would secure UNIVERSAL PEACE, and this grand idea is now an accomplished fact.

1st. He deemed it necessary that explosive projectiles should be made more certain and terrible in their effects than they now are.

2d. That a torpedo should be produced which should be inexpensive and yet *sure to destroy the vessel assailed.*

3d. That magazine cannon, as well as small arms, capable of being fired with lightning-like rapidity, to the extent of 80 *rounds for cannon* and more than 100 *rounds for small arms*, were necessary.

4th. That battery guns which could fire broadsides of 20 to 40 shots at a single pull of the trigger, be effective 2, 3, and it may be 6 miles, and capable of delivering 40 broadsides in one minute, were a necessity.

To accomplish this vast and world wide undertaking. inasmuch as he could not give the required personal supervision to the business himself, Dr. MCLEAN secured the assistance of MYRON COLONEY, formerly of St. Louis, now of NEW

Haven, Connecticut, who was found to possess, in an eminent degree, a profoundly reflective mind and great inventive power, and a MECHANICAL GENIUS of the very highest order. During the late war of the rebellion he had made improvements in cannon, arms and projectiles a study, and upon trial was proved to be fully qualified to carry to a successful issue, the important undertakings confided to his charge.

The result has proven the wisdom of the enterprise, and the revolution in arms, and in the art of war, is an accomplished fact, and he is now able to say to the world, with much more potency than will at once be admitted,

"ALL NATIONS ARE COMMANDED TO KEEP THE PEACE."

Dr. JAMES HENRY McLEAN,

OF

ST. LOUIS, MISSOURI.

THERE are epochs in the world's history characterized by intense expectation—a universal watching, so to speak, for the appearance of some great mind, some giant intellect, capable of giving direction to any reform or revolution which the "signs of the times" seem to indicate is ripe for development and needed to insure true progress in the religious, social and political growth and unfoldment of nations. And when we behold a world or a nation waiting for such a MAN, that man is *sure to be near at hand.* History points out the many grand heroes who have thus suddenly answered the world's longing, and have leaped into the arena of social, political or military activity, and forever stamped their genius, goodness, grandeur and power upon the movements of their time.

In the limits of this brief sketch a few only of the latest and brightest lights, who have made their mark high up in the temple of fame, can be pointed out. NAPOLEON BONAPARTE, first emperor of France and the most brilliant military genius the world ever beheld, caused all Europe to tremble at the approach of his invincible battalions, and to dread the results of his boundless ambition. But at the world's call another great hero arose, General WELLINGTON, whose master mind and unconquerable tenacity of purpose proved too much for NAPOLEON, and forever terminated his brilliant career on the bloody and fatal field of Waterloo. The IRON DUKE permanently established there the supremacy of the Anglo-Saxon race. How well "Old England" has maintained that supremacy, and her just and equitable government wherever she has planted her flag, history faithfully and creditably reports. Descending to later days in Europe, the names of General VON MOLTKE and Prince BISMARCK shine out as stars in the military and political firmament of the German Empire, as men of power, men of destiny, and have indelibly stamped the seal of their wonderful INDIVIDUALITIES upon European history.

In considering the great men of our own country, the mighty Republic of the United States of America, the first name upon her escutcheon is that of the father of our country, GEORGE WASHINGTON, whose military genius led our feeble but determined armies through the trying ordeals of frequent defeats and a long and exhausting war to the glorious end, FREEDOM. WASHINGTON was a NOBLE man, a HERO. He refused to be made a party to defraud the people of the freedom they had so freely shed their blood to win.

During the dark days of our recent civil strife, when our brave men were lying inactive in the Chickahominy Swamps, and perishing from the effects of malaria by thousands, how anxiously and intensely this great nation, and the millions all over the world, who love freedom, waited and watched for "A MAN OF DESTINY," whose masterly skill should mark him as the leader of our million soldiers; a great captain who could so handle our vast armies as to crush out rebellion and firmly and forever establish the bulwark of our liberties. Again the call of the world was answered, and the man of destiny appeared in the person of General ULYSSES S. GRANT, who more than justified all of the demands made upon him, and who has been twice elected to the highest position of the nation, and honored, in his recent triumphal tour of the world, by all of the rulers of the earth. No other man ever received such distinguished receptions from every nation, as

General ULYSSES S. GRANT, the great military genius of the United States.

Again the eager, anxious world is peering through the mists of the future, waiting and watching for another coming man, who, by the power of his great intellect, the force of his determined purpose, may stay the onrushing tide of tyranny and bloodshed, and prove to be A SAVIOR AND LIBERATOR OF HIS RACE. Such a man is the subject of this sketch, Dr. JAMES HENRY MCLEAN, of St. Louis, Mo., whose name will soon be heralded from one end of the earth to the other, and who will undoubtedly prove to be an instrument in the hands of ALMIGHTY GOD of fulfilling the Bible prophecy respecting the millennium period, when "*swords shall be beaten into plowshares, spears into pruning hooks and the nations shall learn war no more forever!*" Dr. J. H. MCLEAN'S WONDERFUL PEACE-MAKERS will compel every nation, great and small, to refrain from invasion, perfect their defenses, preserve their own integrity, and submit all differences to international arbitration.

Dr. JAMES HENRY MCLEAN was born in Scotland, in the year 1829. When a few months old, his father emigrated to Nova Scotia. In that terribly cold but healthful climate he secured that great vital strength and power which sustains the great demands on his wonderful brain. At thirteen years of age he left home to mark out his own course of life, refusing to follow his father's mechanical and geological calling. The boy of thirteen, seeing in the future the vast thousands upon thousands of frontier emigrants and settlers in the West and South suffering from malarial and other diseases incident to all new countries, and the sick and suffering far away from medical aid, resolved upon a career which from the first he carried out with the same will and determination that has ever marked his onward and upward course in life, never flinching from trials, troubles, or difficulties. His

DR. J. H. McLEAN'S OFFICE AND LABORATORY,
314 CHESTNUT STREET, ST. LOUIS, MO.

Medical and Surgical education was completed in the St. Louis Medical College, where his remarkable perseverance and ability were known and recognized. Thoroughly educated also in pharmacy, he was fully capable of furnishing the sick and suffering with prepared remedies, accompanied by plain directions for use, of great value and efficacy.

Dr. J. H. McLean's Strengthening Cordial and Blood Purifier, with his other prepared medicines, can now be found in drug stores in nearly every village, hamlet and home in the Western and Southern States—in fact, in many places in Europe as well as the United States—accessible to the poor as well as the rich. That humane mission fully accomplished, that great life work carried out, one might think would be sufficient; but the Doctor's great heart burned to go on—go on to do more for his fellow-men. Hearing of the killing and slaughter of the brave soldiers in Europe and Asia at the will of their rulers, he resolved to develop such terribly destructive weapons of war, arms, torpedoes, and fortresses, and such perfect defenses, as would compel all nations to keep peace towards each other.

"Save the Lives of the People" is his Motto.

In pursuing his professional career unaided and alone, he amassed a large fortune. The people of the Mississippi Valley know well Dr. J. H. McLean's Grand Tower Block, and his vast Laboratory. With him to will is to do and to have done, having all the means necessary at his command, and the brain and vital force to carry out his enterprises. He has succeeded in developing, and now presents to the world, the most terribly destructive weapons of war, from a 48-shot pistol and 128-shot rifle (self-loading) up to cannons of all grades; Battery Guns, capable of firing from 600 shots a minute up to 2,000 shots a minute, and sweeping an area of six miles; Infantry and Rifle Protection Forms; Floating and Permanent, *absolutely impregnable* Fortresses; swift-sailing

Dr. J. H. McLean's Grand Tower Block,
Cor. Fourth and Market Sts., St. Louis, Mo.

vessels, which cannot be sunk by perforation; and, to complete the circle, a HYDROPHONE, capable of warning ships and forts of the approach or vicinity of hostile vessels; of warning ships at sea of the proximity of icebergs or their nearness to rocky coasts in foggy weather. How many lives will be saved by that simple, though ingenious instrument!

When the world has fully realized the grand success of the crowning act of the life of Dr. JAMES HENRY McLEAN, whose portrait forms the frontispiece of this book, we think all will acknowledge that he *is* truly a Man of Destiny—a great REFORMER in the highest sense of the word, and a savior of the tyrannized and down-trodden human race. "So mote it be."

MYRON COLONEY.

MYRON COLONEY.

ONE of the fundamental errors of a personal government is the belief in the sacredness of the few when compared to the masses. The King, the Church, and the nobility are declared to be the only representatives of the Trinity on earth, and in them resides and from them must proceed all power, all favor, all titles, all renown, all religion, and all things whatsoever of value to the human race. The masses are regarded by them simply as beings designed to minister to their wants; to plough for them, sow for them, reap for them, and, at their sweet will, to march out into the field of battle and be shot for them.

A nation's wealth consists of its people, and is made up of various classes: producers, which are the creators of wealth; consumers, hoarders and dispensers of money. Which class is of the greatest value to the human race? Undoubtedly the producers and creators of wealth.

Among the most important creators of wealth, in any nation, are the inventors. They are the pioneers in merchandising, in mechanics, and in the arts and sciences. One class of ingenious men invent a new, forcible and impressive method of making known their business and of selling their wares, and thereby secure wealth for themselves and afford a means of livelihood to their employees. Other inventive minds, of a mechanical turn, perceive defects in mechanism, and, thereupon, originate new devices which cheapen cost and increase production. Both of these classes, in their way, are creators of the wealth of a nation.

There are others, and greater inventors, who, with one master stroke of genius, wipe out all past works of a class and create instead better and more useful forms, which, in their application, give employment to the many, and contribute to the general prosperity of the nation. The effort of their genius may be directed toward improvements in the tools employed in husbandry, or toward the perfection of machinery for the manufacture of textile fabrics, or in an effort to create more powerful engines of war. Whatever may be the bent of their effort, the achievement is the same. The world is astonished at the result, and then commences to make use of the improvements, and carries them forward to ultimate perfection, employing the labor and the skill of thousands.

To this class, we think, belongs MYRON COLONEY, one of the inventors of the Dr. J. H. McLEAN Peace-Makers, and whose portrait heads this sketch. We predict that ere long the nations of the world will recognize the true merit and importance of these terrible instruments of destruction, which, from the very terror they are calculated to inspire, are well named "Peace-Makers," and that thousands upon thousands of artisans, mechanics and laborers, who will, in their manufacture, be afforded employment, will recognize Dr. J. H. McLEAN, of St. Louis, and MYRON COLONEY, now of New Haven, Conn., as true creators of wealth for the masses. Besides these there will be many thousands more who will rejoice that these wonderful inventions have been perfected in our own country.

MYRON COLONEY evidently derived a great part of his genius from his father, JAMES B. COLONEY, who was born in Keene, New Hampshire, and who, in the prosecution of his trade as a cabinet maker, in Akron, Ohio, to which place he had removed, after the subject of our sketch was born, invented, constructed and used the first turbine water-wheel ever made in the United States.

MYRON COLONEY was born in St. Lawrence county, New York, on the 24th of April, 1832, and when still quite young, exhibited great constructive skill and mechanical ability in building boyish saw-mills, apple-paring machines, animal traps, &c., of curious and novel workmanship. Amongst those rich traits of character with which he was endowed, there was also a deep love of literature. This desire grew almost into a passion, and determined the young lad to enter a printing office, rather than follow his father's more successful trade.

He served an apprenticeship in the *Summit Beacon* office, Akron, Ohio, and subsequently became a writer of acknowledged ability, acting as financial and commercial editor of the *St. Louis Democrat* for many years. Thousands of people in St. Louis are familiar with the arduous and important duties which were required of him on the editorial staff of that largely circulated cosmopolitan journal, and also know the golden opinions and hearty commendations he secured from the merchants of that great commercial and industrial metropolis, who, in a meeting called for the purpose, publicly presented him with a massive gold watch and chain, as a memento of their esteem, respect, and appreciation of his valuable services as a writer, and his able advocacy of the progressive interests of St. Louis and its vast tributary country, the great South, West, and North.

During the late war of the Rebellion, MYRON COLONEY made the defects in our weapons of war and projectiles an anxious and earnest study. Then the ingenious mechanism for firing time shells was invented, and the breech-loading cannon was thought of, both of which are now developed and perfected.

Describing this firing mechanism and breech-loading devices to Dr. J. H. McLEAN, who is not only an eminent physician and surgeon, but also an inventor, MYRON COLONEY discovered he had met a man who had arms and torpedo devices of his own to be developed; and who possessed also brilliant administrative and executive ability, capable of solving the greatest national problems of this age, together with all the money at his command necessary to carry out any undertaking. His great mind had already conceived the vast, grand, and truly philanthropic work of making such terribly destructive arms, torpedoes and projectiles, as would compel the world to keep the peace.

MYRON COLONEY engaged at once with Dr. McLEAN, and removed to New Haven, Connecticut, where he could obtain the best skill and the most able and intelligent mechanics, to superintend and develop those terrible engines of destruction, which are intended to strike terror to the heart of every enemy. Not only those devices, which Dr. McLEAN and Mr. COLONEY then planned, but other great inventions, which his fruitful inventive brain suggested and which he has since perfected, have been called into being, and which will create an enthusiasm and a sense of security in every nation on this globe, handing down to posterity the name of MYRON COLONEY, in connection with Dr. J. H. McLEAN's Peace-Makers, with the greatest honor and credit.

THE ART OF WAR.

In the expressive phrase of the southwestern States of this country, "to get the drop on another" is the true art of war. That is, to be able to kill one's neighbor without being killed by him. A fastidious writer might, perhaps, have written "enemy" instead of "neighbor," but there is no difference in fact. War is a barbarism, and will prevail upon the earth to a greater or less extent until the percentage of barbarians in all nations becomes much reduced. Since each nation possesses a sufficiently large proportion of barbarians to make war at all times possible, and since its evils extend themselves to those who are not barbarians and who abhor strife, it should be made so direful in its results to those who are immediately engaged in it, as to fill the human mind with horror, and make the raising of armies more and more difficult.

General Q. A. GILLMORE, in his report of operations on Morris Island, S. C., in 1863, says, on page 23: "*The best and steadiest troops can seldom be made to advance under the fire of even a few well-served pieces of artillery.*"

May we not conclude, therefore, that it would be very artful warfare to provide arms so deadly in effect that *no* troops could be found to face them?

Believing that the

SUREST METHOD OF MAKING PERPETUAL PEACE

is to make the destruction of armies and navies certain, Dr. J. H. McLEAN has spent a great deal of time and large sums of money in endeavoring to provide the necessary destructive agents to insure this consummation.

He felt that it was not enough that the foot soldier should be provided with a deadly rifle, or that the artillerist should have a greatly improved cannon. The entire list of death-producing machinery ought to be greatly improved; nay, more—revolutionized.

Men ought to be more certainly slain behind fortifications; iron-clad war vessels more inevitably destroyed, and columns of infantry more surely annihilated than is now the case before an effect upon the human mind impressive enough to insure universal peace, could possibly be produced.

Some nations are stronger upon the water than upon the land. This is true of Great Britain. By the power of her naval armament, she has controlled, to a greater or less extent, every nation of the earth. Any power that can successfully and swiftly destroy her iron-clads must and will reduce her supremacy.

Russia is immensely strong upon the land, yet the poor quality of the arms furnished to her soldiers in their recent war with Turkey made the issue problematical for a long time.

WHAT GEN. GILLMORE SAYS OF FORTS.

Gen. GILLMORE says that "forts are only intended to forbid the passage of hostile naval forces into our harbors and up to our arsenals, cities and depots, but are not expected to prevent the landing and moving of troops beyond the reach of their guns. *As at present constructed*, forts cannot sustain land attacks, but can successfully resist and repel the most formidable vessels."

The operations of the "Army of the South," under command of Gen. GILLMORE, against Fort Wagner and Fort Sumter, assisted by a powerful iron-clad fleet under command of Admiral DAHLGREN, off Charleston, in 1863, led to the above conclusion.

Fort Sumter was bombarded by the Morris Island batteries of Gen. GILLMORE's command, for seven days; also by the iron-clads during the same length of time. The land batteries hurled 5,009 projectiles at the fort in that time, weighing 552,683 pounds! The number and weight of projectiles hurled at Sumter by the fleet are not given in this report, but in one of Admiral DAHLGREN's messages to Gen. GILLMORE during the siege, he states that he expended more than half of his ammunition and fully three-quarters of the endurance of his guns on Sumter.

THOUGH DESTROYED IT WAS NOT SURRENDERED.

Yet Sumter was not taken. Its walls of masonry were mashed into a shapeless heap, and its guns were dismounted and a large number of its garrison killed, yet neither GILLMORE nor DAHLGREN could compel a surrender, for it could not be successfully operated against by a large land force. It was surrounded by water and could only be approached by boats. A determined garrison, though but a handful, could make such an attempt too costly to be practicable.

Fort Wagner, a powerful earthwork, and much better calculated to withstand a siege than Sumter, was evacuated after enduring but a two days' bombardment. It was situated on Morris Island, and Gen. BEAUREGARD, who commanded the Confederate forces at Charleston, was well aware that after Wagner's guns had been dismounted by the bombardment of Gen. GILLMORE's batteries and Admiral DAHLGREN's fleet, Gen. GILLMORE would pour his whole army over the walls of Wagner and capture it; therefore, to save the garrison and as much of the material as could be carried away, Gen. BEAUREGARD wisely ordered the evacuation.

Forts, however, may be made impregnable to both land and sea attack, if it is deemed advisable. Caissons may be sunk in any harbor, or coffer dams established and granite foundations laid for forts up to the low water mark. From the water's edge upward, as high as it is necessary to build, the walls of the fort may be of iron; six feet thick, if necessary, all over. There is no limit to the thickness of the iron casing, as is the case where a ship is to be armored.

The fort may be made absolutely impenetrable, and just as impossible to be taken by land as by sea. It is only a question of cost.

THE Dr. J. H. McLEAN'S IMPREGNABLE FORTRESS.

Dr. McLean, having carefully considered the subject of fortifications, as constructed both in this country and Europe, concludes that if any government really desires impregnability, it may be attained by an outlay of money not very much greater than is now spent upon fortifications. But masonry will not do. Iron alone can be made to accomplish the object sought, and no matter how powerful the engine of destruction liable to be brought against it, the impregnable fortress designed by Dr. J. H. McLean, and illustrated in the following pages, will successfully resist the attack. Neither land nor sea force can compel it to surrender. It is designed to sustain a siege for an indefinite number of years, and can inflict dreadful punishment upon any fleet that dare approach within the stroke of its long range Hercules Guns. The illustration on page 28 exhibits the fort in time of peace, and that on page 29 shows it stripped for action.

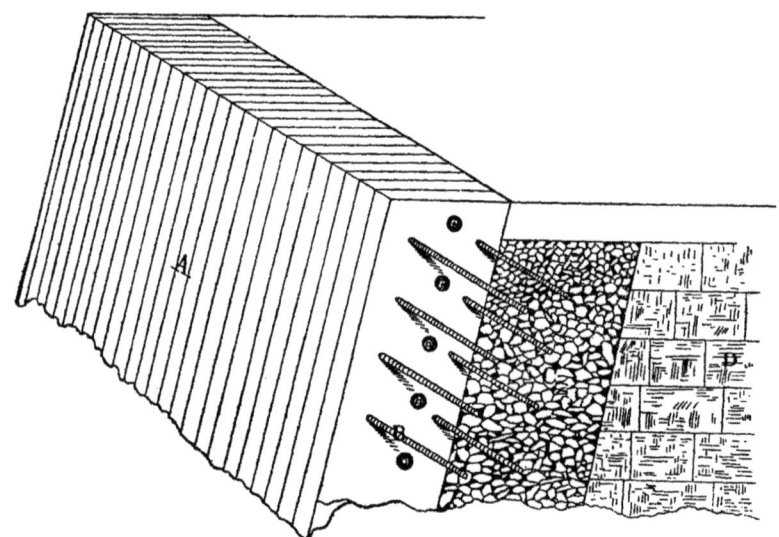

ILLUSTRATION OF DR. J. H. McLEAN'S IRON ARMOR, PRESENTED EDGEWISE TO THE SHOT AND BACKED BY BROKEN STONE.

The engraving on the preceding page, is intended to show the method of constructing the wall of one of Dr. J. H. McLean's permanent impregnable fortresses. First, is the iron armor, set on edge and bolted, as shown, in such a manner that no bolt heads can be cut off by the impinging shot. The armor is backed up by six feet of broken granite; this in turn resting against either a granite wall or a wall of iron plates stayed by braces.

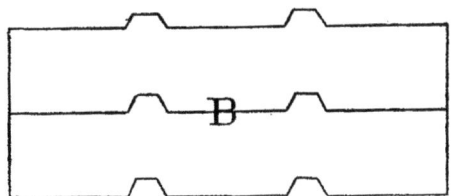

Key Plates for Closing the Gap in the Armor—Top View.

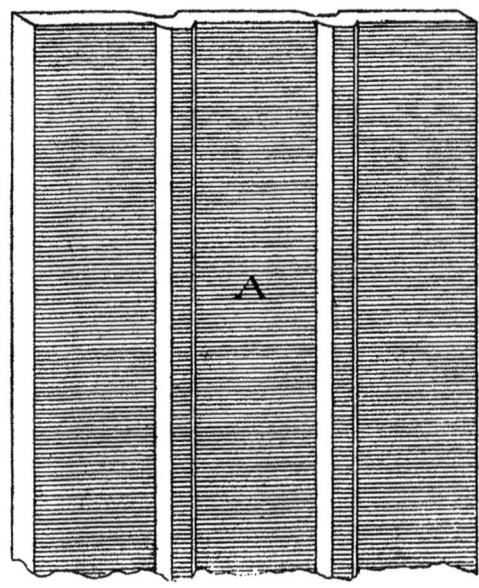

Broadside View.

The Dr. J. H. McLean Impregnable Iron Fortress in Time of Peace.

The Dr. J. H. McLean Impregnable Iron Fortress Cleared for Action.

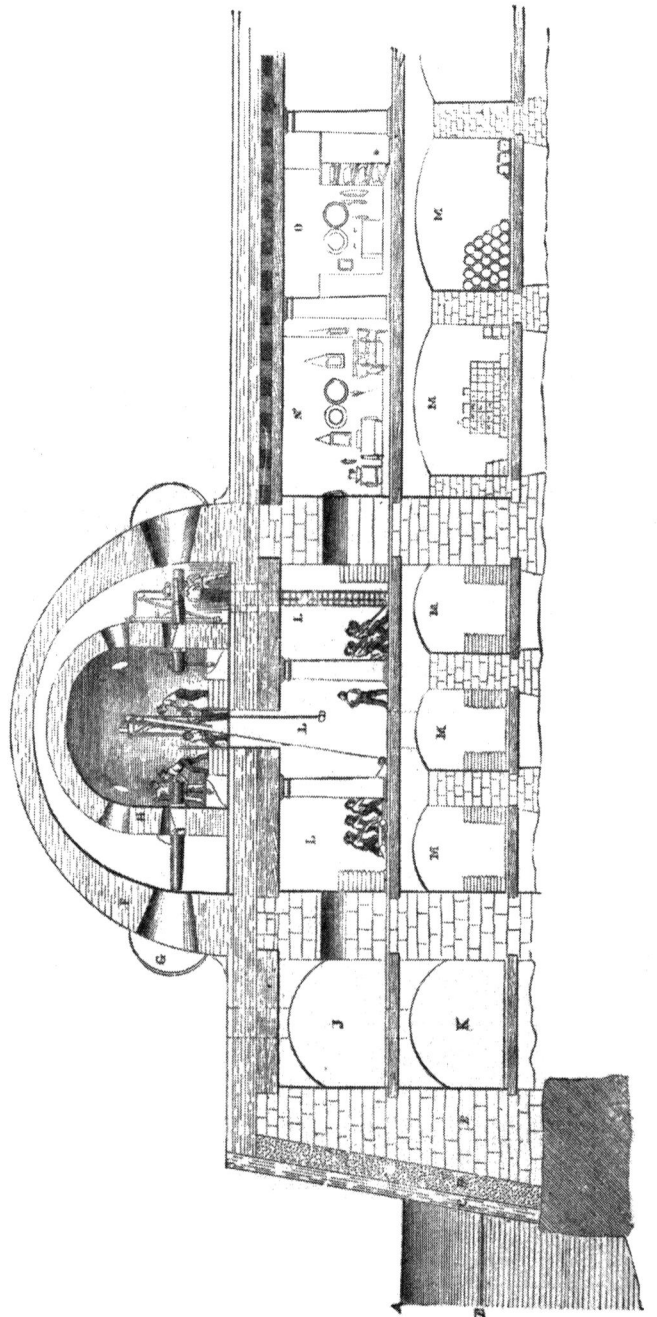

SECTIONAL VIEW OF THE DR. J. H. McLEAN IMPREGNABLE IRON FORTRESS.

A.—High water mark.
B.—Low water mark.
C.—Iron armor set edgewise.
D.—Broken stone backing.
E.—Granite walls.
F.—Wall of outer turret, which is stationary.
G.—Steel jaws protecting port-holes.
H.—Wall of inner turret which revolves.
J.—Engine room.
K, L, M.—Store rooms.
N.—Officers' rooms.
O.—Men's quarters.

It is obvious that as the plates were put upon the bolts as shown in the illustration of them, there would be a point reached, in the progress of the work, where there would no longer be room to insert the bolts, and this gap could then be closed by plates of iron tongued and grooved upon their flat surfaces, as shown in the two diagrams on page 27.

Dr. J. H. McLEAN'S FLOATING IMPREGNABLE FORTRESS.

To have devised an impregnable fortress for permanent construction, would have been exceedingly creditable to any man, and would have satisfied the ambition of most men, but Dr. J. H. McLean foresaw that to succeed in his self-imposed task of compelling men to stop butchering each other, he must cover the entire ground of attack and defense, and that it was quite as necessary that absolutely impregnable floating fortresses should exist, as that permanent ones should be called into being.

In the evolution of a plan for such a fortress, he considers that he has achieved quite as pronounced a success as in the plan for a permanent one. The engraving on page 33 represents a sectional view.

DIMENSIONS OF SUCH A FORTRESS.

Three hundred feet square is suggested as the proper dimensions for such a fortress as is proposed in the illustration. It is proposed to furnish it with a large central turret, the inner one 50 feet in diameter, and the outer one 100 feet in diameter. The lower three tiers of rooms to be 8 feet in height, and the upper tier 15 feet in height. One room on each corner to be open to the sea, and to have hollow cylinders of iron descending from the upper rooms to them, as shown in the illustration, down which cylinders the anchor chains would pass. All the submerged portion of the fort to be constructed of rolled iron less than one inch in thickness, and the entire interior to be divided up into small, water-tight compartments, thus bracing quite sufficiently the entire structure. As the low-water line is approached, armor should be bolted upon the structure of proper thickness, and finally succeeded by the edgewise plates, six feet in thickness, described in the illustrations of the permanent fortress. It will be found quite easy to back these plates by broken granite, as is shown in the permanent fortresses, by backing the granite with a thin wall of iron plates.

THIS FORTRESS DEFIES TORPEDOES.

Such fortresses will prove to be absolutely impregnable. Torpedoes could not damage them sufficiently to produce any effect upon them, for they would always, when in action, come to anchor in water not so deep that the fortress could be submerged in it, while their 200 feet square of iron bottom would afford a solid foundation to the fortress, were it even possible that it should be sunk by a torpedo. But the great number of water-tight compartments, filled with water, which are supplied to this fortress, as shown in the illustration, will be found an invulnerable bulwark against torpedo action. The water is a backing to the wall of each room, and when the torpedo exploded against the exterior wall, the water in the interior would exercise the same repelling power to the energy of the torpedo which the surrounding sea-water exercised, and the room could not, therefore, be broken into. An empty room could easily be broken into because the air in an empty room is more compressible than the surrounding water, but if the room is filled with water, and fully surrounded by water, then the action of the torpedo upon the iron wall of the room is comparatively harmless.

THE COST OF SUCH FORTRESSES.

Undoubtedly the first objection urged against the construction of such fortresses would be their presumed expense.

Nothing is too dear in time of a nation's peril which serves the end intended, and anything is too dear, however cheap to construct, which fails to do

THE ART OF WAR. 33

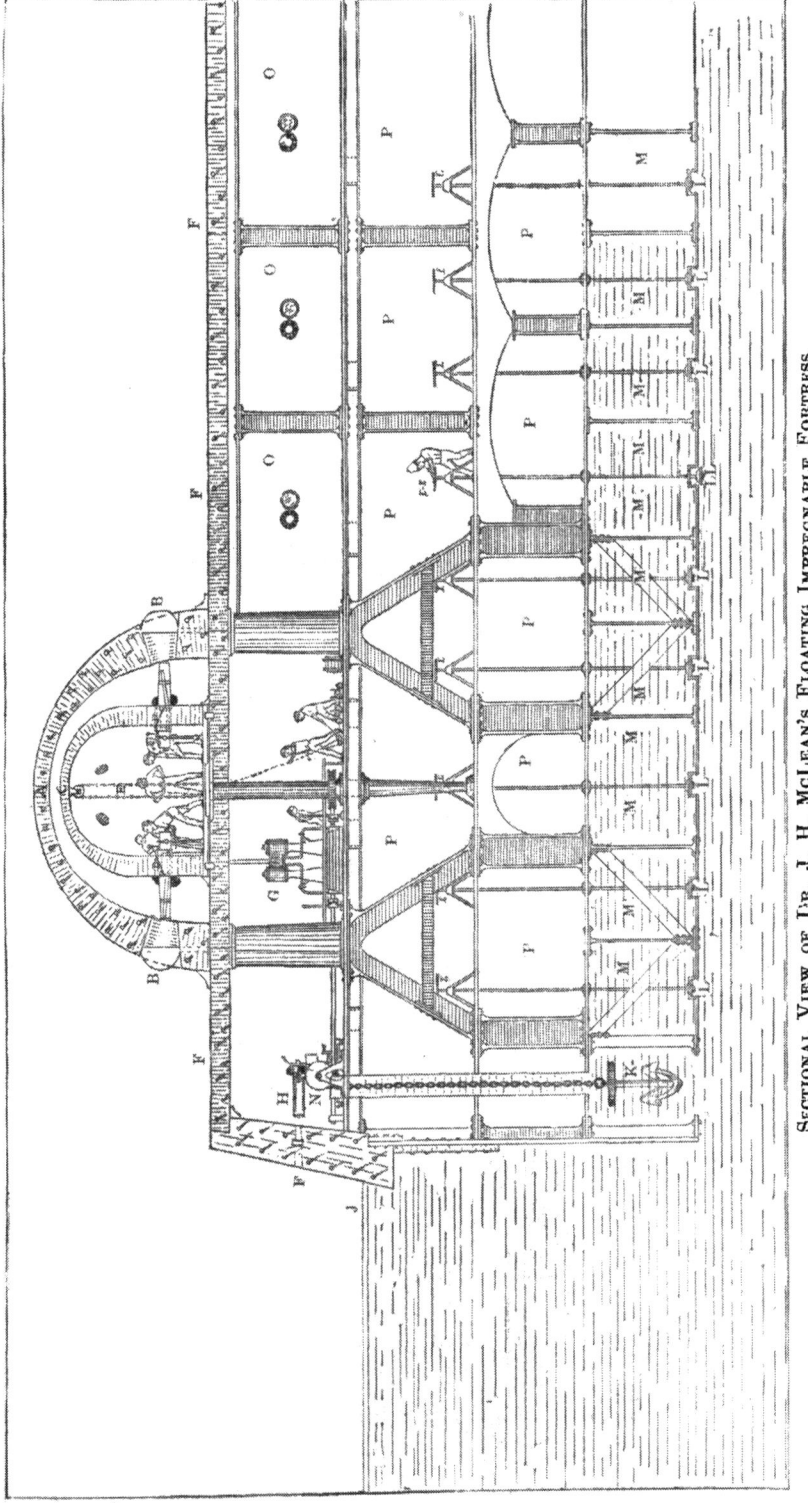

SECTIONAL VIEW OF DR. J. H. MCLEAN'S FLOATING IMPREGNABLE FORTRESS.

A.—Inside and outside turrets.
B.—Steel jaws for closing port holes.
F.—Armor on edge.
G.—Machinery for working turrets, pumps and anchors.
H.—Lady McLean Battery.
I.—Brakes to work the floating valves.
J.—High water mark.
K.—Anchor in each corner of the fort.
L.—Floating valves.
M.—Water-tight compartments, some of which are flooded and some empty.
N.—Windless around which the anchor chain is wound.
O.—Apartments for officers and men.
P.—Store rooms.

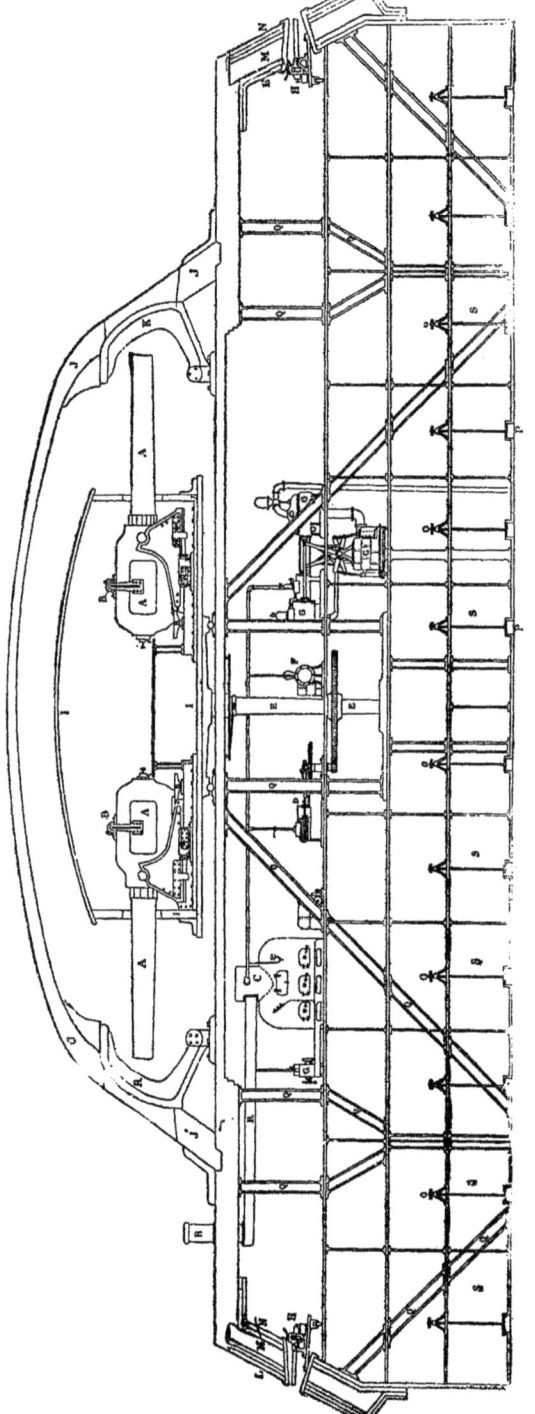

Cross Section Through the Center of Dr. J. H. McLean's Impregnable Floating Iron Fortress, Showing Double Turrets and Two Hercules Guns in Position.

A—Guns.
B—Hydraulic presses for working guns.
C—Boiler.
D—Engine for revolving turret.
E—Turret shaft and gearing.
F—Steam Pump for presses.
G— "   "   water compartments.
H—"Lady McLean" battery guns.
I—Inner revolving turret.
J—Outer fixed turret.
K—Port stoppers.
L—Outer armor, 6 feet thick.
M—Stone backing.
N—Interior casing.
O—Valve hand wheels.
P—Valves.
Q—Braces, Posts.
R—Boiler flue.
S—Water compartments.

THE ART OF WAR.

this. The city of Paris was surrounded by cheap fortifications, and in their last war they proved to be the dearest forts that France ever built, for they failed to keep the German army out of Paris.

Let us sum up the cost of these wretched forts to France:

1st.	Indemnity to Germany	$2,000,000,000
2d.	Cost of the war	1,000,000,000
3d.	Loss of territory	5,000,000,000
4th.	Loss of life	1,000,000,000
5th.	National humiliation	5,000,000,000
6th.	The Commune	1,000,000,000
	Total	$15,000,000,000

Since her humiliation France has thoroughly reorganized her army, spent millions of francs in new weapons, and has constructed a new line of defenses around Paris at a cost of one hundred millions of dollars, yet not one of the forts which she has now constructed at so much cost and labor is impregnable. With the one hundred millions of dollars expended, a belt of Dr. J. H. McLean's impregnable permanent iron fortresses, 500 feet square, supplied with 5 turrets each, mounting a total of 10 one-hundred-ton Hercules guns to each fort, might have been built entirely around Paris. When this is done France may defy all the powers of earth to take Paris, but not until it is done will this gay Capital of the world be absolutely safe from the invasion of its foes.

DETAILS UNNECESSARY.

It is quite unnecessary to enter into the full details of the construction of the fortresses herein proposed. It is sufficient to state in a general way that Dr. McLean is fully posted as to the best means of building them, their cost, the best means for ventilating, lighting and storing them for a siege. All such points are easy of accomplishment. The main thing is to prevail upon the various governments of the world to adopt them. Army and navy commanders are the principal advisers of the stern military governments of the old world, and these people are not progressive. They occupy a fixed position in the world; they have been trained in deep and rigid grooves, and lack incentives sufficient to enable them to discard old and familiar methods of thought and action, and assume new and strange ones. They have been taught to consider their own positions and persons wholly superior to the positions and persons of non-military people, and to admit that civilians could evolve from their commoner clay any ideas or inventions of value to the superior intellect of the army and navy would be; in a measure, to stultify their assumptions of superiority.

American officers are not quite so hide-bound as those who are alluded to above.

The experience of Gen. GILLMORE, on Morris Island, compelled him to say:

"The development of modern artillery require corresponding modifications in the engineer's art. Progress must be met with progress; art confounded with art; science set against science."

It is much easier for a commanding officer in the American army to arrive at so true and creditable a conclusion than it would be for a similar commander in any of the military governments to do so, because the American commander mingles more with the people of the nation than the other does, and becomes inoculated with their progressive spirit, and our people are, as a class, more fertile in inventions than those populations who are repressed and intellectually restrained by the compressing force of a strong military government.

ONLY DISASTERS TEACH SUCH PEOPLE.

When their armies are slaughtered by weapons which they have scornfully rejected, or they waste their strength and substance in vain attempts to reduce a fortification built contrary to the red-tape prescriptions of their schools, they are apt to wake up to a consciousness that their vaunted "system" does not comprise all of the possibilities of progressive warfare.

SUPERIORITY OF THE DOUBLE TURRETS.

As yet turrets have only been used in the construction of armored ships and small floating batteries, and for such purposes the weight of a single turret of 4 to 6 inches thickness has been found about all the ship or battery could well sustain. A ship 250 feet long, at first thought, seems to present an immense bulk for the displacement of water, but when its shape is considered, and the further fact that it would not exceed 40 feet in width, the vast superiority of the flat-bottomed fortress, 200 feet square, as a buoyant mass, becomes clear. Upon the deck of this fortress may safely be imposed the two great turrets provided for in the foregoing sketches.

It is proposed that the inner turret shall be 50 feet in diameter; that two of Dr. J. H. McLean's hundred-ton Hercules guns shall be mounted in the wall of this turret, said wall to be four feet thick.

It is proposed that the outer turret shall be 100 feet in diameter, 6 feet thick, stationary, furnished with 8 or more port-holes guarded by steel jaws of adequate strength.

As the inner turret revolves, the jaws are automatically opened whenever a gun is in line to deliver its shot. That the automatic mechanism for insuring the opening and closing of the jaws as described, be under the immediate management of the commander, so that any or all of the jaws can be thrown out of or into gear with the mechanism at his pleasure.

THE TERRIBLY STUNNING EFFECT

of the impact of immense projectiles upon the exterior of the thin wall of a single turret can be adequately realized by few excepting those who have had to endure it. The men in the double turret have no such dreadful experience to undergo. The hammering of the missiles upon the thick, large outer turret could not affect them unpleasantly, and in perfect comfort and absolute security they could work their large guns at will. Neither would they be

TROUBLED WITH THE SUFFOCATING GAS

which sweeps into the single turret through the large port-hole necessary to it. The great gun in the single turret fits into its wall snugly, only a peep-hole for sighting the piece would afford an avenue for the inward passage of the gas, so that, practically, the air in the inner turret would be as sweet and salubrious as that obtainable upon the deck of a ship. While large steel bows bend over the port-holes in the outer turret they do not close them; consequently there would always be a strong and free passage of the air all through the interior of the outer turret, and keep the gases in such rapid motion that little if any could penetrate the inner turret.

Dr. J. H. McLEAN'S HERCULES GUNS

are especially adapted to these turrets.

First. Because they are breech-loaders, and the men in the inner turret would not find it at all difficult to load them.

Second. Because the barrel screws into the breech, hence several duplicate barrels could be kept in the space between the two turrets, and were it to chance that a projectile should enter the port-hole and break one of the gun-barrels, that gun would not be disabled more than 10 minutes, for in that time the broken barrel could be unscrewed and a perfect one screwed into its place. It would be of little use to build double turrets and mount muzzle-loading guns in them, for the greater portion of the force required to serve them would have to be collected in the space between the two turrets, around the muzzle of the gun, exposed to the horrid din, the smoke, gas, and entrance of missiles through the port-hole.

Dr. J. H. McLEAN'S IRON FORMS.

If Dr. J. H. McLean, in the whole course of his very busy and useful life, had produced nothing more useful to the world than his Iron Forms, for the rapid construction of forts, bomb-proofs, bullet-proof tents for the wounded, bullet-proof sheds for horses and mules, and perfectly secure breastworks for battle lines, he would still be entitled to the thanks and gratitude of mankind. These Iron Forms are capable of being pressed into such a variety of uses, that the army which has once tried them will wonder how it ever got on without them. The following illustrations exhibit the Iron Forms and a few of the numerous uses to which they may be put:

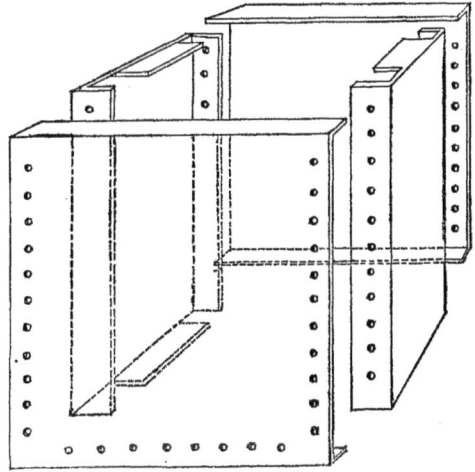

The Dr. J. H. McLean Iron Form in Parts, to be Riveted together.

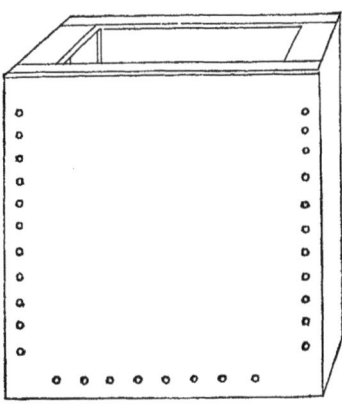

The Dr. J. H. McLean Iron Form Riveted together.

Dr. J. H. McLEAN'S HINGED IRON FORMS.

The above illustration exhibits the Iron Forms in four parts, and these parts to be made useful, must be bolted together, but the following illustrations show the same parts *hinged together*, and the reader will be informed of many uses to which these admirable forms can be put:

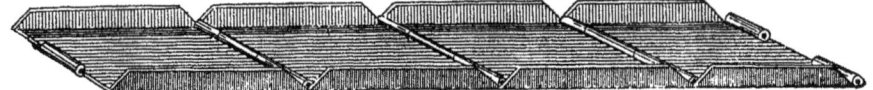

Dr. J. H. McLean's Hinged Iron Form laid down flat.

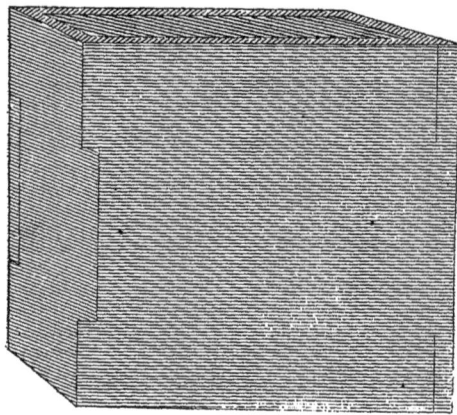

Dr. J. H. McLean's Hinged Iron Form shut up, forming a Box.

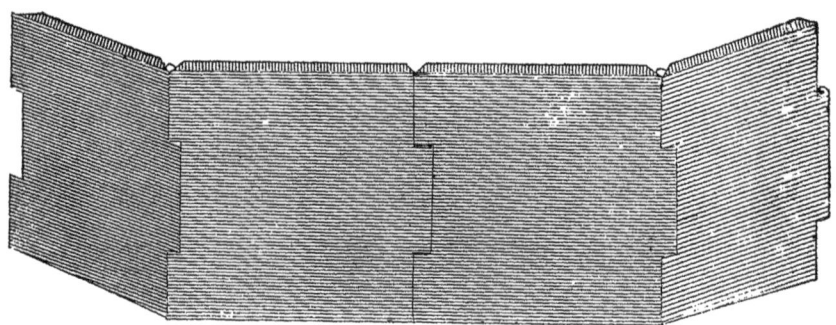

Dr. J. H. McLean's Hinged Iron Forms standing on edge, forming a Segment of a Wall for a Battle Line.

Dr. J. H. McLean's Hinged Iron Forms hinged together in a Continuous Wall to protect a Battle Line.

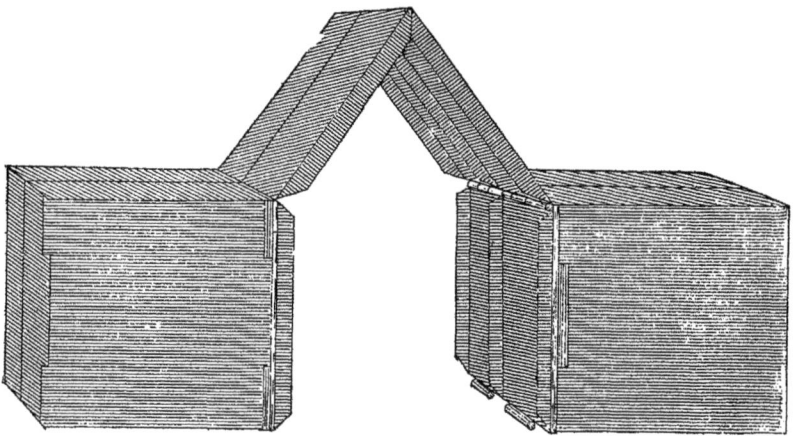

Dr. J. H. McLean's Iron Forms set up to form a Section of a Bullet Proof Tent.

THE McLEAN HINGED IRON FORMS AS TETHERING AND FEED BOXES.

Shut up into boxes, these invaluable iron forms may be used in ordinary camps for feeding and securely tethering the stock. The plan now pursued in the U. S. army, is to stretch a long heavy rope between two stakes, and to this rope the mules and horses are hitched, head to head. The fodder and grain is then put upon the ground along the line, and much of it is wasted; but a few of the admirable McLean Hinged Iron Forms might be shut into boxes and stretched along in a line. Halters could be passed through the loop holes in the boxes, and they could then be stuffed with hay. The flanges upon the edges render the aperture at the top smaller than the inside diameter, which would be a favorable circumstance, as it would tend to prevent the mules or horses from pulling the hay out too freely and wasting it under their feet. The weight of the forms would insure a more secure tethering of the stock than is offered by a line stretched between stakes.

THE IRON FORMS USED AS COOKING RANGES.

The hardships of a soldier's life are many, and his pleasures and comforts few, so that anything which may be devised, which will not only contribute to the safety and success of an army, but to the comfort of the soldier as well, ought to meet with universal encouragement. In rapid marches, in pursuit of a fleeing or in retreat from a victorious enemy, privation, and even a verging upon starvation, is endured without much grumbling, but in camps of protracted stay, and upon marches where loss of time is not an important factor, the comfort of the men should be studied. Properly cooked food is one source of immense comfort, and in a camp where all of the fires are built upon the ground and exposed to the sweep of the wind, food cannot be properly cooked.

It would be the work of but a few seconds, to draw out of a wagon belonging to the mess department, a couple of Dr. J. H. McLean's Hinged Iron Forms: one to be closed, forming a large iron box, and the other to be stretched over the top of the closed one.

An admirable cooking range has thus been called into being in a moment, the loop holes affording places over which to place pots and pans, and an ingenious management of two more of the boxes will form a large baking oven, with one side of the boxes to swing as a door.

Dr. J. H. McLEAN'S HINGED IRON FORMS IN THE INDIAN SERVICE.

The recent sharp conflict (Oct. 28, 1879) between the U. S. forces under the command of the Late Maj. THORNBURGH and the Ute Indians, at Milk River, Colorado, is so fresh in the minds of the people of this country, that the efficacy of Dr. J. H. McLEAN's Hinged iron Forms, had they there been in use, will be apparent by the following extract from Capt. PAYNE's report of the battle:

ON THE SKIRMISH LINE.

"With a quick and soldierly perception of the situation, Lieutenant CHERRY turned back and made signals for the command to retrace its steps. Just as the leading company (F, Fifth Cavalry) was descending a ridge into the valley beyond, Company E was immediately conducted to the side of the hill on its left flank, while Company E of the Third Cavalry was halted on the high ground it occupied, and both companies at once dismounted and deployed, by Major THORNBURGH's orders, as skirmishers, Company E of the Third Cavalry on the right along the crest of the ridge, and F Company of the Fifth Cavalry as well up the side of the hill, which, constantly ascending, stretched away indefinitely, as the nature of the ground would permit. Our line at this time resembled the letter V, the points toward the Indians, and that portion of it formed by Company F, Fifth Cavalry, projecting considerably beyond the point of junction, and being deflected to the left so as to prevent the enemy from turning our flank."

THE INDIANS OPEN FIRE.

"At this time attempts were made, by Major THORNBURGH in person and by Lieutenant CHERRY, to communicate with the Indians, but efforts in that direction were met by a shot, and at once a hot fire was opened on us and the fight began all along our lines.

"The Indians had displayed admirable skill in the selection of the ground upon which to give us battle, and it was soon apparent that our position in the face of the enemy, superbly armed and greatly our superior in force, was untenable."

FALLING BACK.

"With sound judgment and a quick and thorough perception of the situation, Major THORNBURGH determined to form a junction with Company D, Fifth Cavalry, which was protecting the wagon train, and with that end in view directed the companies engaged to fall back slowly. The command retired, as directed, in perfect order, the led horses being kept well protected between the skirmish lines of the two companies, while a heavy and effective fire did great execution among the savages, and prevented an attempt on their part to break through our lines. Failing in their efforts in front, the Indians endeavored to cut the command off from the train, which had, by Major THORNBURGH's order, gone into park on the right bank of the Milk River; and, to accomplish this purpose, passed around our left flank beyond the carbine range, and concentrated in great force upon a knoll to the left of, and completely commanding our line of retreat. Major THORNBURGH, upon discovering this new danger, directed me to charge the knoll with twenty men of my company, and to sweep the Indians off; and then, at once, without attempting to hold the hill, to fall back upon the train and take measures for its protection. This duty being performed, and the way opened for the return of the led horses, I repaired to the wagon train and at once took steps looking to its defense."

MAJOR THORNBURGH KILLED.

"Major THORNBURGH, doubtless, started for the train shortly after giving me the order referred to, and was shot and instantly killed just after crossing the river, and within 500 yards of the wagons. His gallantry was conspicuous from the first to the last, and grief for his death was general and profound."

AT THE WAGON TRAIN.

"In the meantime, Captain LAWSON, with E Company of the Third Cavalry, and Lieutenant CHERRY, with a detachment of E Company of the Third and F of the Fifth Cavalry, gallantly held the Indians in check in front, gradually retiring,

Lieutenant CHERRY with his detachment covering the retreat. Upon reaching the train I found it parked on the right bank of Milk River, about two hundred yards from water, the wagons forming the north side of a corral, elliptical in shape, its long axis running east and west, and the south side exposed to a fierce fire from the Indians, who, massing in the ravines along the river and upon commanding heights, were making a determined effort to capture and destroy the train before it could be placed in condition for defense."

SLAUGHTERING MULES AND HORSES TO MAKE BREASTWORKS FOR THE MEN.

"The animals were crowded in the area indicated, and I at once directed some twenty or more of them to be led out and shot along the open space referred to, thus making continuous our line of defense, and affording cover for our sharpshooters.

"As soon as these arrangements were completed, the men were ordered to unload the wagons, and use bedding and grain and flour sacks for breastworks. I cannot speak too highly of their conduct at this time. Though exposed to a galling fire by which many men and horses were stricken down, they worked with alacrity and courage, and in a short time our corral was in as good a state of defense as the means at hand would permit. About this time Lieutenant PADDOCK, who was encouraging the men by the exposure of his person, and intelligently and courageously carrying out my instructions, was wounded in the hip. As Captain LAWSON and Lieutenant CHERRY, whose gallant fight in covering the retreat deserves high commendation, had not returned to camp, I became solicitous for their safety, and detached Sergeant POPPE of my company, with twelve men, to proceed down the road in the direction from which they were approaching. In a short time thereafter I was greatly relieved at seeing Captain LAWSON and Lieutenant CHERRY, with their commands, enter the entrenchments. A new and critical danger now threatened us."

FIRE AND SMOKE.

"The Indians, foiled in their efforts to prevent the concentration of the command at the train, or to drive us out of it by a furious and concentrated fire, took advantage of a high wind blowing directly toward us, and fired the tall grass and sage brush down the river. At the moment this peril was realized, I observed that the Indian supply train of Mr. JOHN GORDON was parked within seventy-five yards of my position, and so situated as to command our approach to water. Seeing this, and fearing that, under cover of the smoke, the Indians might make a lodgment in this train, which, in my judgment, would have been disastrous to the command, and with the further view of burning the grass on the north side of the corral, to present as little surface as possible to the Indian fire when it should approach, I directed the grass on that side to be fired, and in a few moments was gratified to see GORDON's train in flames. The fire from down the valley approached with great rapidity, and struck the exposed part of the corral, * * * and for a few moments threatened us with destruction. The officers and men at this critical moment, when the Indians made their most furious attack, displayed superb gallantry. Several lives were lost and many wounds received, but the fire was extinguished and our greatest danger passed."

FEARFUL SLAUGHTER OF THE POOR ANIMALS.

"From this time (about a quarter to three, P. M.) until nightfall, the Indians kept up a furious fire, doing great damage to our stock, fully three-fourths of them being killed or so severely wounded that they were killed by my order. At dark a large body of Indians charged down behind Gordon's burning train, delivering volley after volley. They were repulsed easily and fled, suffering the loss of several warriors, who were distinctly seen to drop from their saddles. During the night our dead animals were hauled off. A full supply of water for twenty-four hours was procured; the wounded were cared for; entrenchments were dug, and by daylight the corral was in a good condition for defense. Couriers were sent out with despatches at midnight, and a general feeling of confidence inspired the entire command. Ammunition and rations were distributed in the several trenches, and I felt that sense of security for my command, which sprang from a knowledge of its gallantry and fortitude."

ALL OF THE MULES KILLED EXCEPT FOURTEEN.

"During the next day the Indians kept up an almost incessant fire, killing all of our animals but fourteen mules, but doing no other damage. We were unmolested the night of the 30th, but after that time the enemy gave us no rest. During the night of the 1st our water party was fired upon at short range, and one man of F. Company, Third Cavalry, was shot through the face. The guard for the water party returned this fire with effect, killing one Indian."

THE GALLANT COLORED RESCUERS.

"On the morning of the 2d, Captain Dodge and Lieutenant Hughes, with Company D, Ninth Cavalry, came into our camp, adding materially to our fighting strength, and bringing the welcome news that our couriers had gone through safely. I cannot express in too high terms my appreciation of the gallantry of these brave officers and men, and it is peculiarly gratifying to know that they have received the praise which such courage richly deserves.

"Colonel Merritt, with his command, after a march which has no parallel, reached us this morning, and were received with hearty and prolonged cheers by my gallant men, whose patriotic fidelity and courage were thus speedily rewarded by rescue from great and impending peril. I can find no suitable words in which to express my admiration for the officers and men of my command. Their conduct was beyond all praise. They were gallant under fire, patient during suspense, and confident through all. It is my greatest pride to have commanded them, and to know that one more page in the glorious annals of the American soldier has been illustrated by their valor.

"J. SCOTT PAYNE,
"Captain Fifth Cavalry, commanding."

A FEW WAGON LOADS OF Dr. J. H. McLEAN'S IRON FORMS,

hauled along with Major THORNBURGH's command, would have saved the great sacrifice of life and property detailed above, and would not have cost the government as much money as the mules cost which were shot to make breastworks of. Look upon the engraving on page 47, and realize how differently that fatal battle might have resulted. The mules and horses are then sheltered completely by bullet-proof coverings, the men are equally well protected and are armed with Dr. J. H. McLEAN's magazine rifles, and have one of the terrible Lady McLEAN battery guns to use upon the enemy.

SAVE THE SOLDIERS' LIVES.
THE IRON FORMS MADE INTO BOXES FOR LINES OF BATTLE.

Dr. J. H. McLEAN takes the high and humane ground, that the lives of soldiers should not be needlessly sacrificed.

"A victory is twice itself
When the achiever brings home full numbers."

Therefore, whatever ingenuity can devise which shall, without encumbering the movements of an army too much, increase its effectiveness and very greatly diminish its mortality, should be freely and gladly accepted and introduced by all governments. In Indian warfare, where only rifle balls are to be encountered by the soldier, the hinged iron form stretched into a breastwork will be found sufficiently effective, but where the forces of a civilized power are to be confronted, grape, shell and cannon shot must be taken into account.

Though but few men are ever actually slain by cannon shot, shell or grape, yet the fact that the soldier encounters a constant liability to be thus slain, is more or less demoralizing.

THE ART OF WAR. 47

Dr. J. H. McLean's Iron Forms Converted into Bullet Proof Shelter for Stock and into Breastworks for the Men.

AN UNNERVED AND EXCITED SOLDIER

is not in a condition to do good execution in battle, though he may, by the severe discipline of the service, be kept in line; but a soldier who is in a position of comparative security from cannon shot, grape and shell, feels quite at his ease, and will not only refrain from an excited and senseless waste of his cartridges, but he will fire with wonderful deliberation and accuracy, and one hundred men so circumstanced will create greater havoc in an enemy's line than double the number who are compelled to stand up in close order and fight according to prevailing tactics. And the one hundred men behind the boxes, as shown in the following engraving, will not use more than a quarter of the ammunition in doing the greater service which will be used by the two hundred men in doing the lesser service, and the casualties among the one hundred men will not be one-tenth of the casualties among the two hundred men.

NON-EFFECTIVENESS OF ARTILLERY AGAINST THESE IRON BOXES.

As before stated, artillery seldom slays men. Occasionally a soldier is struck by a cannon shot, but when lying behind even the crudest covering, the liability to be so struck is greatly lessened, and the soldier lying behind one of the iron boxes filled with earth, shown in the following illustration, is almost absolutely safe from such a casualty. Not but that a cannon shot *might* penetrate the box and kill the man behind it, but that it *ever will do so* is as little likely as that lightning should strike the man instead. A cannon shot coming toward the line of boxes, describes an arc of a circle. If it strikes the box before it does the ground, it will penetrate the first thickness of iron obliquely; the earth in the box will aid in retarding the progress of the shot, and also be instrumental in confirming its oblique direction, and it would emerge from the lower corner on the opposite side, and plunge into the earth beneath the soldier.

Should the shot strike the ground before it reached the line of boxes, it would ricochet and pass entirely over them, and this would probably be the case with ninety-nine shots out of every hundred aimed at the line.

THE ART OF WAR. 49

Dr. J. H. McLean's Iron Forms made into Boxes and filled with Earth, as Breastworks.

Indeed, the position of an army intrenched, as shown in the illustration, behind Dr. J. H. McLean's Iron Forms made into boxes, and supported, as also shown, by a line of "Lady McLean" Battery Guns,

WOULD BE FOUND PRACTICALLY IMPREGNABLE,

and any opposing army that rashly ventured to storm such a line, would be well nigh annihilated; for the men are armed with Dr. McLean's formidable magazine rifles, capable of delivering one hundred and twenty-eight shots as rapidly as the trigger can be pulled, and they are supported by a line of Dr. McLean's terrible battery guns, known as the "Lady McLean." These guns discharge a level broadside of forty shots at a time, an inch and a half in calibre, and can throw two thousand of them in one minute.

Before such a hellish blast nothing could live an instant. Even forests would be swept to splinters, while men and horses would be cut down like grass before a mower.

QUICK WORK: MAKING THE BOXES INTO FORTS.

It frequently happens that the fate of a campaign depends upon holding certain strategic positions. In such an emergency Dr. J. H. McLean's Iron Forms are beyond all value. As pontoons have frequently saved an entire army from destruction, by enabling them to cross intervening rivers in their rear, when hotly pursued by a victorious enemy, so these iron forms are capable of changing the fate of an entire campaign, of converting defeat into victory, and of preventing the humiliation of a nation. The following illustrations will make themselves clearly understood:

Converting Dr. J. H. McLean's Iron Forms into a Fort.

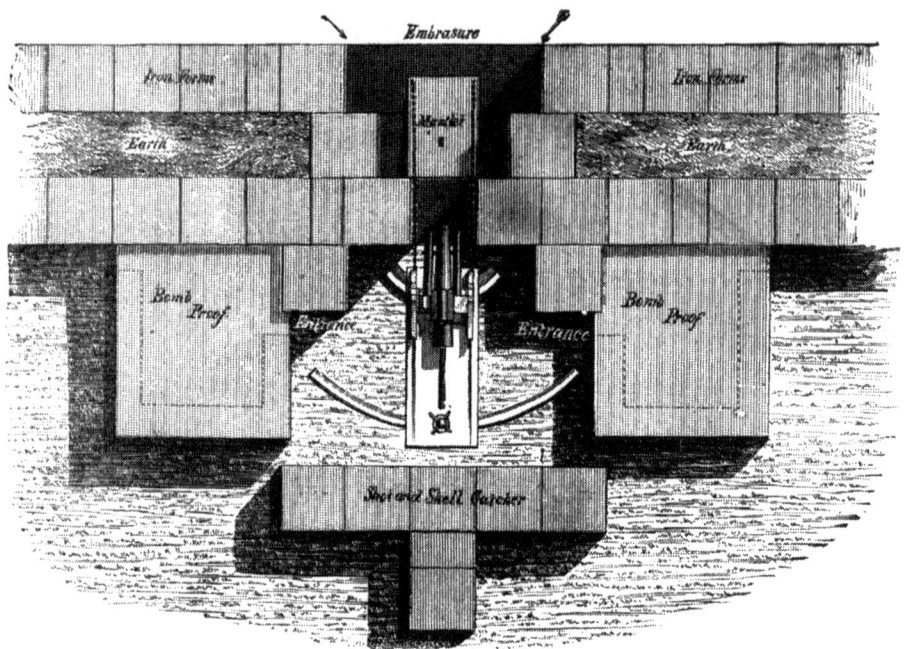

VIEW OF A SECTION OF THE FORT; LOOKING DOWN UPON THE TOP OF IT.

THE IMPREGNABILITY OF SUCH A FORT

consists in the inability of the enemy to reduce its walls, or encumber its embrazures with debris. The above sectional view of the fort is worth a close examination.

First, it will be seen that there are an outer and an inner wall of iron forms, the space between being filled with earth. The boxes are also filled with earth, and are laid up like a wall of masonry. Cannon shot will puncture but will not shatter these iron boxes as masonry is shattered, and the weight of the boxes allow of their being pierced without being disturbed in their positions. They are made of thin boiler iron to insure that very result, hence none of the embrazures will be encumbered with debris after a bombardment, as is the case in forts built with gabions, sand bags, and earth or masonry. An iron mantlet, swung on chains attached to the gun carriage, so as to be closed by the recoil, is shown in the engraving. This mantlet is made of thin iron, and is only intended to protect the gunners from sharpshooters. Bomb proofs, constructed out of the iron forms, are shown to the right and left of the embrasures. These apartments afford secure quarters for all of the men not needed to work the guns. In the rear of the gun will be seen a collection of iron forms put up in the shape of a T, entitled "Shot and Shell Catcher." The shot and shell of an attacking enemy are mainly directed against the embrasures of a fort, because there the men are sure to be collected: the offensive points of a fort are there, and the guns are there to be dismounted. A shell or shot entering the embrasure is caught by this device of Dr. McLean's, and is prevented from doing farther mischief. If it be a shell and bursts inside the boxes, no harm will be done; if it be a shot, it is prevented from crossing to the other side of the fort and doing damage to the men or guns upon such side.

CROSS-SECTION VIEW OF THE EMBRASURE OF A FORT MADE WITH DR. J. H. McLEAN'S IRON FORMS.

One of Dr. J. H. McLean's magazine cannon is shown mounted in the embrasure of this fort, and should a shot enter the embrasure, strike this cannon and tear away part of its muzzle, the barrel can be unscrewed from the breech in five minutes, and a duplicate substituted. Therefore the gun would not be silenced.

Of what other gun can this be truthfully written?

EXTERNAL APPEARANCE OF THE FORT AFTER ENDURING A PROLONGED BOMBARDMENT.

The above illustration is undoubtedly a fair representation of the external appearance of such a fort after it had submitted to a prolonged bombardment: full of holes, but unchanged in form. Every shot which struck would cut a clean round hole through the thin iron of the box, and plunge into the earth beyond. No boxes would be knocked away from their positions; and the earth firmly rammed into the boxes, would not run out of the shot holes. Hence the walls of the fort would present a smooth and undisfigured face, not much like the appearance of the REDAN after its evacuation by the Russians in the Crimea, as shown by the illustration on page 55

The REDAN was a Russian fort in the Crimea, attacked by the allied armies of England, France and Turkey, in 1850. Its walls were composed of earth and stone, and its embrasures were rivetted with gabions and sand-bags. Its bomb proofs were also built of gabions and sand-bags; and it was considered a very formidable and well-nigh impregnable fortification, and it defied the combined and concentrated attack of all three armies for many days. But it was finally knocked to pieces. Its badly-mounted guns were dismounted, its em-

APPEARANCE OF THE REDAN AFTER ITS EVACUATION BY THE RUSSIANS.

brasures crowded with debris, and its bomb-proofs were broken down, so the Russians abandoned it—a useless ruin to its captors. Everything of value was carried out of it, and our illustration is a faithful copy of a photograph taken by the military an hour after it was evacuated.

It will be observed that the embrasures of the Redan were provided with *rope mantlets*, to shield the exposed men at the guns from the French and English sharpshooters; but the entire superiority of Dr. J. H. McLean's hastily constructed fort must be conceded.

The Redan is a type of all forts constructed by non-progressive military skill. It took a long time to build it and no small sum of money, yet it was valueless when finished.

MAJOR DELAFIELD'S TRIP TO THE CRIMEA.

Major J. R. Delafield has written an elaborate work entitled "Art of War in Europe," and which consists principally of matter founded upon his observations in the Crimea. Several extracts from that work are transferred to these pages, with a view of strengthening the general arguments as advanced by Dr. J. H. McLean, in the preceding pages and in those to follow:

CONSTRUCTING BOMB PROOFS.

"There was no rest or safety for the soldier, except under cover of some expedient or other which should shelter him from bombs. Great labor and persevering industry was bestowed upon temporary expedients for securing a night's rest undisturbed by shot and shell. In the Redan were seventeen apartments six feet square, hewn out of solid rock, capable of sheltering three men each—the excavation of which must have cost a deal of hard, persistent and resolute labor."

CASEMATES.

"The difficulty of giving vent to the smoke, has always been set forth as one of the greatest objections against casemates. It has been completely set at rest, and repeated experiments have proved, that their fire can be as rapid as may be obtained from artillery elsewhere. * * * But this objection overcome, it is argued that the exterior smoke, hanging over the ditches contiguous to the embrasures, becomes so dense as to prevent aiming, and renders the fire inefficient from the darkness created in the casemate. While this is denied, it is at the same time true that an open battery would be liable to the very same inconvenience, as it is constantly enveloped in its own smoke. On shipboard, with low decks, and the men's heads near to the ceiling, smoke sometimes accumulates so as to be troublesome, yet no serious inconvenience arises.

THE INSTINCT OF THE SOLDIER TO SHIELD HIMSELF.

"The gabion is a cylindrical basket open at each end, with pointed upright sticks projecting from the ends to keep them in place and prevent slipping. A soldier would place one of these gabions in front of him, between himself and the enemy, and fill it with earth dug from under his feet. He then rapidly digs a trench, while protected by his gabion, throwing the earth on the outside, between the gabion and the enemy, and thus in a few minutes has a ditch deep enough to give him pretty good protection from the enemy's grape shot."

USE OF THE IRON FORMS FOR BATTLE LINES.

"During a night the Russians would make small lunettes, covering from ten to twenty men, and in other places barely sufficient for the cover of a single individual. These small works took the name of rifle pits. The smaller ones, in some instances, were mere piles of loose stone, collected and thrown together sufficient to conceal a man lying down; others were formed of two gabions laid end to end, forming an obtuse angle, *filled with stone or earth*. These rifle pits were located beyond the influence of the allied artillery, covering individuals and small parties of infantry, firing on workmen in the allied trenches, heads of saps and unfinished batteries. Some of them were in deep ravines, under batteries into which the artillery *could not be depressed*. This mode of defense certainly *was unusual*, and only to be practiced with troops who are individually inspired with the cause of their country. These rifle pits, simple as they appear, were so formidable as to resist several attacks of the French, and were only taken on the 22d of March, by a powerful night attack, by 12,000 French troops."

OBSTRUCTING THE HARBOR.

"The day the allied army moved on Sebastopol from the Alma, the Russians commenced to guard the entrance into the harbor. Seven large ships (five of which were two-deckers, the other two frigates) were sunk at the entrance into the harbor, on a line of not less than seven hundred yards in length, leaving their mast-heads generally above water. Whether seven ships on a line of that length, and in from four to ten fathoms water, formed an impassable barrier, the nautical reader can easily determine."

"* * * The lesson is one for our consideration. For years past we have expended no greater sums on a seacoast fort than an individual expends in the same time, in many instances, for his residence; and more than one occasion has passed when an enemy, with a knowledge of our neglect, could have done us as great damage as Russia sustained from a similar neglect. In our case, however, it has heretofore been from apathy and indifference to the subject of *national defense*, and not the want of time or resources, as in the case of Russia."

NECESSITY OF PREPARATION FOR WAR IN TIMES OF PEACE.

"The permanent defenses, constructed in time of peace, were equal to their object against every combined, permanent preparation of the allies. In a resort to expedients, constructed in time of war, the combatants were on equal terms, both parties being enabled to provide with corresponding rapidity. Under like circumstances, with the immense resources of our own country, our ability to provide auxiliary seacoast defenses would be as readily accomplished as those of Russia, provided we are prepared against armaments existing at the commencement of hostilities. Such means are then reliable against the fleets of Europe; but when accompanied by armies, as at Sebastopol, we shall see that additional means become necessary to effect the same security, which Russia had not the time to perfect, and hence lost a city, a fleet and dockyards."

FORTIFICATIONS.

"The reliance upon fortifications, both for the defense of harbors and road-steads against fleets, and of depots, arsenals and strategic points on frontiers, appears greater, and their value more appreciated at the present time than ever. * * * All the military science and experience of Europe coincide in opinion of the necessity for fortifications at strategic points, depots, dockyards and arsenals."

EFFICIENCY OF ARTILLERY.

"Artillery fire is, with the continental engineers, more relied upon than infantry. Gen. TOTLEBEN, the engineer of Sebastopol, constructed most of his defenses so that the approaches to them should be commanded by distant as well as near artillery fire."

TENDENCY TO BUILD BIG GUNS.

"This enlargement of calibre has, since the period of our revolution, been steadily on the increase, especially in the fleets of all nations. Eighteen and twenty-four pounder guns, once common in the armament of frigates and even ships of the line, are now totally abolished; the eight-inch gun being a common substitute.

"The lesson to be derived from these facts on the increased size of European artillery, should cause us to lose no time in *substituting the like* for the twenty-four and thirty-two pounders on which we at this moment mainly rely.

"I may bring to notice another fact in the armament of our seacoast batteries, that late experience requires we should not overlook. On many of our narrow channels we have adopted the eight-inch chambered gun, for such comparative short ranges and for *hollow shot only* (shells?). We now know that floating batteries, protected by an armor of four and a half inches of iron, can cross the Atlantic, and are proof against thirty-two pounder solid shot, and eight and ten-inch hollow shot; but, at a distance of four hundred yards, the eight and ten inch *solid shot* will pass through the armor, or break away its fastenings."

BAD GUN CARRIAGES AND CASEMATES.

"We labor at present under difficulties in the armament of our seacoast batteries by the universal adoption of *timber chassés and truck carriages*. Our wooden carriages are not only liable to rot, but, in both casemate and barbette, are subject to such frequent changes from warping, as to render entire batteries unfit for service. *In some cases the chassés will rest on three wheels;* in many, the centre stock is so twisted that the *upper carriage is liable to be thrown off, dismounting the gun whenever the recoil brings the gun to the rear of the chassés;* and, in but very few instances that have passed under my notice, is the prop, at the end of the centre rail of the chassés, *such as to take any bearing whatever on the platform.* * * * Russia has adopted *wrought-iron chassés and carriages for both garrison and seacoast batteries.* To her practice, in this particular, I invite the attention of the secretary of war."

Dr. McLEAN'S POSITION PROVED.

It is plain, that every position taken in these pages by Dr. McLean is well taken. Major Delafield acknowledges the absolute need of sheltering the men, and in response to this need, Dr. McLean offers his iron forts. Major Delafield concludes that casemates are all right, and Dr. McLean offers casemate protections for his big guns in the impregnable double turrets of his forts. Guns of light calibre are declared to be practically useless. Dr. McLean offers his 100-ton Hercules guns. Forts constructed of sand-bags and gabions, are shown to be vulnerable. Dr. McLean offers forts constructed from iron forms, which cannot be knocked to pieces.

Dr. J. H. McLEAN'S IMPROVED IRON WAR SHIP.

The development in the weight and power of projectiles has been so extraordinary during the past few years, that invulnerability of armor for vessels has not been able to keep pace; and it has happened that while a ship, supposed to be able to resist the impact of the most formidable missile known, was in course of construction, a gun has been meanwhile built capable of riddling her with ease; and it is probably true that no ship exists to-day that could not be speedily knocked to pieces by the hundred-ton guns now in use.

These guns can send their projectiles through twenty-four inches of solid iron, and such an armor is too weighty for ships to carry and remain seaworthy, and to be easy to manœuvre.

But suppose a vessel can be constructed which could carry safely and well an armor of six feet in thickness, and be fully able to resist the shot of the heaviest guns ever likely to be built, what would be gained when a single torpedo can send her to the bottom?

Dr. J. H. McLean believes it to be wise to change front entirely upon the question of war ships, and instead of seeking to

KEEP OUT THE ENEMY'S SHOT

by defensive armor, to rather construct a vessel which will not be greatly damaged if even the largest shot go clear through her. He has, therefore, caused the whole subject of shipbuilding for offensive purposes to be considered by competent minds, and has also given the subject a careful personal consideration, and the sum of his conclusions are as follows:

First—A ship to be superior to any now known as a *fighting ship* must be SWIFT.

Second—She must be capable of being handled with great ease and readiness; able to turn round in a circle of a diameter not more than twice her length.

Third—She must be divided into numerous water-tight compartments.

Fourth—She must be built entirely of thin iron.

Fifth—She must be able to resist the shock of torpedoes and be fitted to use both the submarine and the projectile torpedoes against an enemy.

Sixth—Her pilot-house and commander's lookout must be made perfectly invulnerable to shot.

Seventh—She should carry but four guns, but they should be of the largest calibre and most perfect accuracy.

Dr. J. H. McLEAN BELIEVES HE HAS JUST SUCH A SHIP

mentally constructed, and submits to the world the section on page 62.

That the mind of the reader may fairly take in and fully retain all of the admirable points claimed for a vessel that shall be constructed as proposed by Dr. McLean, in the foregoing sketch, the following detailed explanations are deemed advisable:

SHE SHOULD BE AN IRON SHIP THROUGHOUT.

Light, perfectly rolled and sound boiler iron to be used in her exterior covering and internal partitions. The hull to be subdivided into numerous and irregularly placed compartments, to be constructed of the same thin iron as the outside covering, and to be made perfectly water-tight in every particular. By making these compartments small, the ship will be greatly stiffened and strengthened; and should one of them be broken into by a shot below the water-line, comparatively no damage would be done, even were the compartment to fill with water.

By placing these compartments irregularly, the partitions are made to "break joints," so to speak, and the power of resistance to the impact of shot or the force of a torpedo is much increased.

A torpedo, exploded beneath a vessel so constructed, would rupture several of the lower compartments beyond a doubt, but not enough of them to seriously cripple the ship, much less to sink her.

Thin iron is advised, because the boat will thus be made light, and, by the numerous partitions, she would also be staunch and able to cope with any sea.

The use of wood in any part of the vessel is not deemed advisable, because wood is both dangerous and useless.

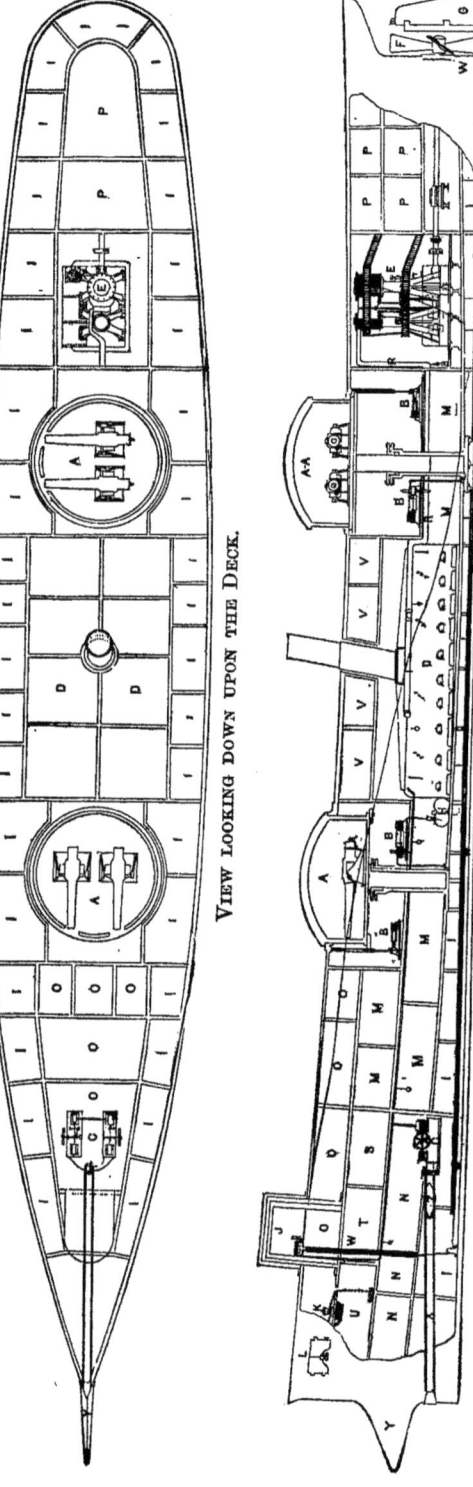

View looking down upon the Deck.

Dr. J. H. McLean's Improved Iron War Ship.—Elevation.

AA.—Turret elevated for firing, armed with two of Dr. J. H. McLean's Hundred Ton Hercules Guns.
A.—Turret before its elevation for firing.
B.—Turret engines for revolving and elevating.
C.—Compressed-air torpedo engine for throwing submarine torpedoes.
D.—Boilers.
E.—Engines.
F.—Propeller.
G.—Rudder.
H.—Engine blower for furnace and ventilation.
I.—Water-tight compartments.
J.—Pilot-house and commander's lookout.
K.—Capstan and engine.
L.—Anchor port-hole.
M.—Water tight compartments for coal.
N.—Torpedo room and magazine room.
O.—Water-tight rooms for officers.
P.—Water-tight rooms for engineers.
Q.—Steam supply pipe for forward engines.
R.—Main steam supply pipe.
S and T.—Provision rooms, water-tight.
U.—Chain room.
V.—Water-tight quarters for the gunners and crew.
W.—Rudder connections.
X.—Tube through which torpedoes are to be projected.
Y.—Ram.
Z.—Torpedo in tube, ready for projection.

When a shot strikes the iron ship described, it will punch out a clean, round hole in the iron; and if a man is in range of the shot, he will be killed. But a shot entering a vessel backed with wood, drives ahead of it long and dangerous splinters, that kill men entirely out of line of the shot itself. The smooth hole punched in the iron ship can be very quickly stopped by iron discs faced with rubber, prepared beforehand to fit any hole from two to twenty inches; but the jagged hole made through the sides of a wooden ship is difficult to stop, as there may be large cracks extending in many directions from the center of the hole, which cannot be the case with an iron ship.

The pilot-house and the commander's lookout is to be a small turret, made with the Dr. J. H. McLean armor plates set edgewise, interposing a solid iron wall of 6 feet in thickness between these important officers and an enemy's shot.

SAFETY OF THE MEN CONSIDERED.

In action, all of the men would be stationed in positions where there was very little likelihood of a missile ever reaching them. For instance, a portion of them would be in the magazine rooms below the water line, and a portion in the gun rooms, also below the water line and in the center of the ship, so that a shot would have to crush through many of the iron partitions before it could possibly approach the gun rooms.

The same is true of the engine and furnace rooms. They are placed below the water line and in the center of the ship, and would be surrounded by several tiers of water-tight compartments.

This ship is designed to be

NOT A HOLIDAY SHIP, BUT A FIGHTING SHIP,

and consequently there are be no spacious saloons that can be converted into ball rooms, no fancy promenade decks, and no luxurious apartments in which aristocratic commanders can entertain their swarms of parasites at the government's expense.

There would be no formidable looking "gun deck," with rows of old

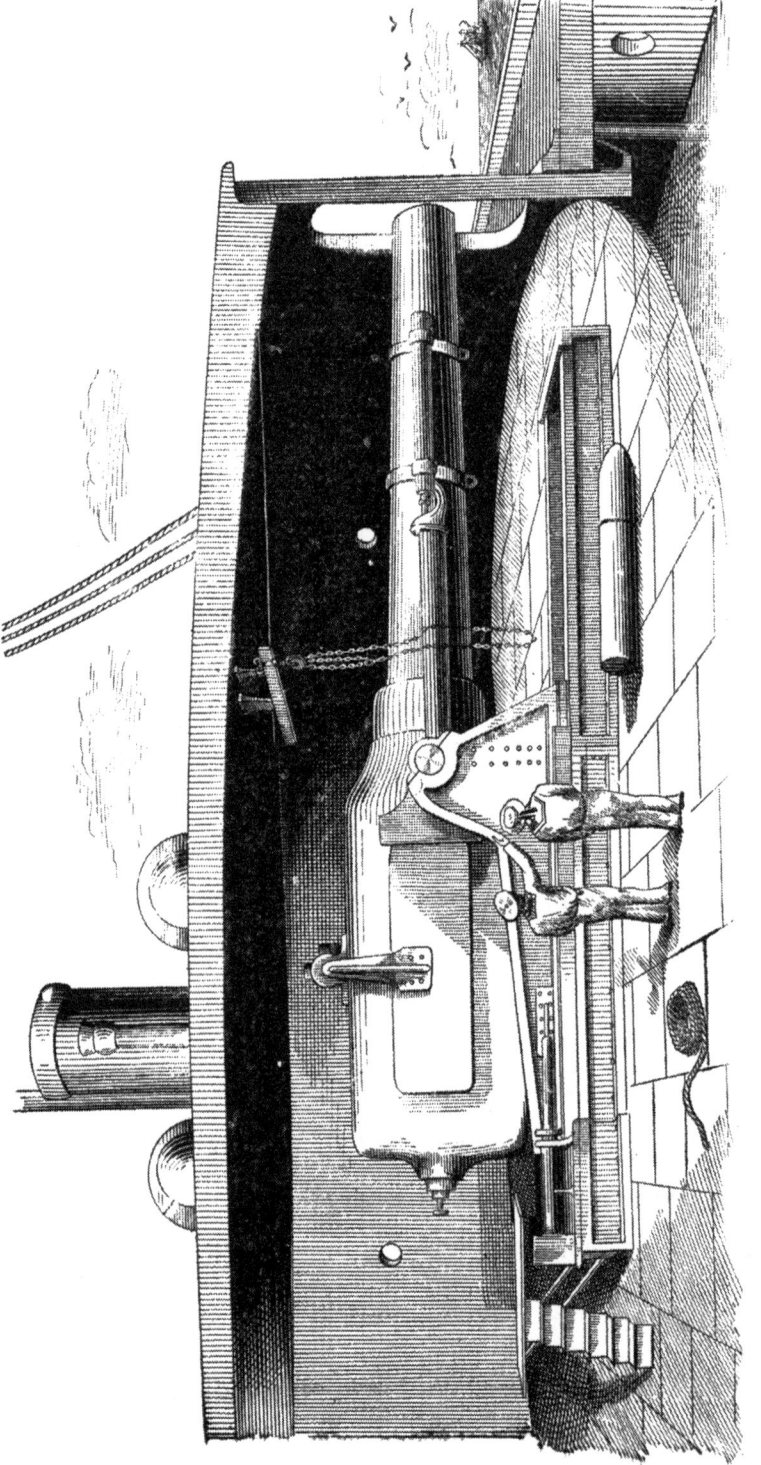

View of Dr. J. H. McLean's 100-ton Gun Hercules, On Board of One of His Proposed Swift Iron Steamers, Elevated for Firing.

fashioned and useless guns thrust out of open ports, and swarming with gunners to furnish easy and appalling food for flying splinters and bursting shell.

No open "gun deck," up and down which excited and stimulated commanders could prance during an action, howling out their commands and brave words under the impression that they were making heroes of themselves.

No. In this ship but few men would be massed together in any particular locality. Compartments would separate the squads, and the orders of the commander, from his secure place in the pilot-house, would be given through the telephone to the orderlies, and reach every compartment in the ship.

To insure a maximum

SPEED OF THIRTY MILES AN HOUR

for such a vessel, when necessary, Dr. McLean has caused a new style of engines and boilers to be invented. These, for obvious reasons, cannot be fully described in this book, but the fundamental plan is to drive the propellers with a much higher velocity than is now done. It is believed the boilers and engines devised for this vessel will easily accomplish the object, and, in addition to this, great improvements have been made by the Doctor in the propellers themselves, which, it is fully believed, will add greatly to the speed of the ship, were there no improvements in the method of generating the steam and in its application to the machinery.

In all matters relating to this great question of national defense, Dr. McLean has insisted upon the utmost thoroughness, and has spared neither time nor money in testing, by research and by experiment, the soundness of his theories, and is ready to be put to the proof upon them by any government on earth. With the records of the past before them, few naval men can be found who would seriously undertake to controvert the positions assumed in the construction of such a ship as is described. If the nation must needs have

HOLIDAY SHIPS AND TRAINING SHIPS

to satisfy the love of display so closely interwoven with military concerns, let an adequate number be constructed, by all means. And the more showy and elegant they can be made, the better. Never intended to be used in war, the guns can be very light, very bright, and very cheap. The decks and saloons can be fitted up sumptuously, and in times of peace such ships will do us infinite credit. But, by all means,

LET US ALSO HAVE THE FIGHTING SHIPS.

Such ships as those proposed by Dr. McLean, can be built at a much less cost than her great Iron Clads have imposed upon England, and one of them would be worth, for actual, effective service, a whole fleet of those cumbersome and ponderous vessels. The speed of such a vessel would enable it to run up to any iron clad and discharge its torpedoes with fatal effect. That the ship would be struck and penetrated by the missiles of its enemy, there can be no doubt; still, little harm would result from the clean cut holes which could be rapidly stopped up. While receiving the shot of the iron clads, the gunners of the proposed ship would not be idle, by any means, but would work their ponderous guns with precision and rapidity, perfectly safe in the meanwhile from the missiles of their adversaries, while from his secure position in the pilot-house the commander, observant of everything taking place, could cooly direct the motions of his vessel, and, by means of the telephone, issue orders to every one on board. But such a vessel armed with any other than

Dr. J. H. McLEAN'S PEACE-MAKERS

would be imperfect, because no guns now manufactured combine all of the essential points which these guns do. They can be worked by very few men, not one of whom, except the pointer, need ever have had any previous training. They are breech-loaders, self-cockers, and furnished with an apparatus to take up recoil, which leaves them always in range after firing. But their full merits will be found set forth in great detail elsewhere in this book.

THE POVERTY OF THE UNITED STATES IN WAR SHIPS, FORTS AND GUNS.

The *Army and Navy Journal*, of April, 1879, contains an article from the pen of the distinguished soldier, Gen. Q. A. Gillmore, entitled, "How shall we defend our seacoast?" of some length and full of solid sense. As many of the statements in this article harmonize exactly with the views entertained and opinions expressed by Dr. J. H. McLean, the entire article is transferred to these pages.

THE COUNTRY WANTS GUNS, FORTS AND SHIPS.

"The official reports of the Chiefs of Engineers and of Ordnance, for the last half dozen years and more, furnish some very significant facts. They show with great force and clearness: (1) That we possess no guns capable of making a good defense against a modern fleet; and (2) If we had the guns, we have no places prepared to mount them in, where they could be effectively served against armored vessels, firing small missiles and case shot at suitable ranges.

"In other words, before we can hope to repel the attacks of war vessels of recent type, not only will the artillery for our forts have to be procured, but the forts themselves will need to be built, or the existing forts greatly modified.

"This statement is so entirely true in all its practical bearings, with respect to the most valuable of our positions on the seaboard, that they may properly be regarded as wholly destitute of suitable protection, that which has been provided for them, by the stringent economies of Congress, being of little, if any, account."

OUR OLD AND USELESS GUNS.

"It is true that we have on hand at our forts and arsenals a number of old mortars, and rifled and smooth-bore guns of obsolete models and insufficient calibres, and the best of them are, or could soon be put, in readiness for such doubtful service as they might be able to render in our barbette batteries, where guns and gunners are in full view, exposed to direct and curved fire. Whether they could be served at all, even for a brief period, in these exposed positions, against vessels showering grape, canister and case shot from large guns, and leaden bullets from machine guns and other rifles, would be a question of the gravest import, were the guns themselves of the requisite calibres and power. They are known, however, to be so entirely unfit for the work they would have to do, as to render it in a great measure immaterial whether they could be served or not. It is not, however, altogether immaterial, for these small calibres would be effective against wooden vessels and light-plated iron clads. An array of them, therefore, would in a degree determine the character, and restrict the number of vessels that could come to the attack with reasonable hope of success. They would be useful for defending harbors accessible to vessels of light draft only.

"It thus happens, since we have a partial supply of small guns and no large ones, that we can make a better defense of our shallow and less valuable harbors than we can of those having deep and capacious channels of approach, so that our ability to protect varies inversely with the importance of the points requiring protection.

"But when the best has been said in our favor, we must still confess that our metal is altogether too light; that our projectiles would fall harmless against modern naval armor; and that any approach to an effective defense, at important points where most needed and most demanded, would be simply out of the question."

THE BEST INVENTIONS OF THE AGE DEMANDED.

"New inventions in gun making, in armor clad ship-building, and in the use of explosives in submarine warfare, have revolutionized the former conditions of defense. Every effort which the means placed at its disposal would allow, has been made by the Engineer Bureau of the War Department, to adapt our existing forts to the new and exacting requirements thereby imposed.

"The following paragraph, in connection with the subject of barbette batteries and a system of defense by torpedoes, is taken from the last annual report of the Chief of Engineers:

"'But torpedo defense, however efficient in itself, cannot stand alone; the torpedoes must be protected by shore batteries. Unfinished earthen batteries, however, provided with a small fraction only of the number of guns for which they were designed, and those of insufficient calibre, and mortar batteries without mortars, though aided by torpedoes, will form but a feeble defense against the powerful fleets prepared and now being prepared to take the high seas. The great powers of Europe do not place their reliance on barbette batteries. They believe in and are constructing casemated forts, some of which are provided with wrought iron scarps, and others with iron casemated shields to protect the gun, and gunners serving it, both from direct and curved fire. This department, while recommending and urging the construction of barbette batteries as an initiatory means of obtaining, by comparatively small expenditures, a partial defense for the numerous exposed harbors of our coast, has always insisted that the efficient service of the large guns mounted in them would require high parapets, and depressing or counterpoise carriages. It has, also, from the beginning, looked forward to the ultimate conversion of some of our casemated forts, which would admit the change, for the reception of guns of the largest calibre, and to the possible construction of new works.'

"It is known that these views are shared by the Board of Engineers for Permanent Fortification, and generally by officers of rank in the Engineer, Ordnance, and Artillery branches of our service."

SUCH FORTS AS Dr. J. H. McLEAN'S IMPREGNABLE FORTRESSES IMPERATIVELY DEMANDED.

"The early completion of suitable defenses for our seacoast frontier would, therefore, seem to be a consideration of the highest moment to the interests of continued peace. National weakness and national danger are interchangeable terms. Indeed, immunity from insult, whether among nations or among men, is largely determined by their ability to resent or avenge it.

"The defenses should be not only suitable with respect to their efficiency, but reasonable with respect to their cost, and should, moreover, as far as possible, anticipate improved means of attack, or be susceptible of ready and inexpensive adaptation to them, so that costly preparations of all kinds, both afloat and ashore, that may be deemed sufficient at the present day, may not, while yet in their infancy, have to be set aside as worthless or inadequate."

SUCH SHIPS AS THOSE PROPOSED BY Dr. McLEAN BELIEVED TO BE BEST.

"The practice of naval construction at the present time unmistakably tends to vessels of moderate draft, eliminating that supposed security against armored fleets which some of our comparatively shallow harbors were formerly, and very properly, thought to possess.

"It seems improbable that many such unwieldy monsters as the 4-gun turret ship *Dreadnought* and the 12-gun broadside ship *Alexandria*, which, together, cost the English government over $5,000,000, exclusive of armament and outfit, will be built in the future.

"Disregarding, however, any additional danger to ourselves likely to ensue from vessels of lighter draft, there are among the present armored fleets of Europe only ten cruisers drawing more than 27 feet of water, and only three drawing more than 28 feet, while there are half a hundred drawing 24 feet or less.

"Depth of draft is not a measure of offensive power. The most powerful batteries may be and are carried on a moderate draft of water. The English turret cruisers *Inflexible*, *Agamemnon*, and *Ajax*, armed with the 81-ton and 38-ton guns, draw but 25 feet, and high naval authority asserts that armored cruisers of a very formidable type can be built on a service draft of 23 to 24 feet.

"There are more than a dozen fine harbors on our Atlantic coast—Portland, Portsmouth, Boston, Newport, and Hampton Roads being among the number—easily accessible on the flood, and affording good inside anchorage at all stages of the tide, to the largest war vessels that have yet been built.

"There are more than half a dozen other harbors, among which may be specified New Bedford, New London, New York and Key West, into which some of the deepest draft men-of-war cannot enter. There is not one of them, however, that does not possess sufficient depth to pass about half the armored cruisers of Great Britain, including vessels armed with the 38-ton and 81-ton guns; all the German armored vessels, except one; more than two-thirds of those of the Italian navy; all belonging to the Russian navy, except two; all belonging to the Austrian navy, except three; all belonging to Holland and Turkey without exception, and a portion of those belonging to the French and Spanish navies."

SITUATIONS IN WHICH Dr. J. H. McLEAN'S FLOATING IMPREGNABLE FORTRESSES WOULD BE INVALUABLE.

"The aggregate population clustered closely about these twenty harbors for armored vessels is nearly three millions, while the value of public and private property exposed within easy and destructive range of a hostile fleet cannot be far short of two thousand millions of dollars. The losses that might be inflicted upon these communities in a few hours, if unprotected, would greatly exceed the entire cost of suitable permanent defenses for the whole country.

"No account is here taken of that incalculable and far greater injury to the country which would be entailed by even the brief presence of a victorious hostile fleet in our waters, keeping the whole coast in alarm, and deranging and destroying the business and industry of the people.

"There is yet another class of harbors, with still shallower channels of entrance, into which a draft of 22 to 24 feet can be safely carried, many of them being the centers of extensive commercial and manufacturing interests. These are exposed to the attacks of the lighter draft iron clads.

"Several of our large and growing cities are at present exempt from the attacks of armored cruisers. Philadelphia, Baltimore, Norfolk, Wilmington, N. C., Charleston, Savannah, Pensacola, and New Orleans belong to this class. The channels leading to some of them are, however, in process of enlargement upon a scale which will place them in the category of localities needing protection against modern fleets.

"It appears, therefore, that our entire Atlantic and Gulf coasts from Maine to Texas, a distance of more than 3,000 miles, is, in the absence of artificial means of protection, peculiarly at the mercy of a hostile naval power, and that our largest centers of population, commerce and manufactures, where the greatest values are accumulated, and therefore where the greatest injury could be inflicted in the briefest interval of time, are within easy reach of the most powerful vessels of war that science, in its far-reaching possibilities, has yet devised. The condition of the Pacific coast is equally defenseless.

"It is presumed that no one will doubt the propriety of providing protection for the great interest thus placed in jeopardy. The question is, what shall be the character and magnitude of that protection?"

THE VULNERABILITY OF OUR SEAPORTS.

"The attack upon our seacoast establishments would be made by a fleet of armored and other steamers, armed with heavy guns and equipped with offensive torpedoes, and probably also with rams, the main object being to destroy our naval establishments, our cities and large towns, or to levy contributions upon them, and, in special cases, as subsidiary thereto, to effect a lodgment in one or more good harbors, and maintain it by naval superiority during the war, as a basis for predatory naval expeditions.

"The elements of seaboard defense constituting a connected system are (1), a regular army and militia; (2), permanent fortifications garrisoned by artillerists and provided with offensive and defensive torpedoes; and (3), a navy provided with rams and offensive torpedoes.

"No army, as such, however well appointed and equipped it might be for active operations in the field, could have any influence upon the result of a naval action in our waters, because destitute of heavy artillery, a requisite factor in such a conflict. Its presence might swell the list of casualties, the same as that of any other interested but idle spectators of a contest in which they could take no part; but no useful result could ensue therefrom.

"If the enemy, however, attempted or succeeded in making a landing upon our coast, in order to march through the country upon his objective point, the duty of defense would fall upon the army and militia, and could be left there with entire confidence. We need not ask for a better guaranty of safety than the circumstance which gives opportunity for the enterprise, courage, and patriotism of our people to display themselves. Such a contingency is specially contemplated in our system, which, by providing local defenses for channels of approach to important points, compels an enemy, as a condition of success, either to land beyond the reach of those defenses, or to attack them by his fleet. In the former case, he would be confronted by the army; in the latter, an army could make no resistance. The question is, in what way can resistance be best offered?

"The essential requisites of a good defense against a modern fleet are heavy artillery, rams and torpedoes, and trained men to manage and use them. A suitable array of these would constitute the local defenses referred to."

HOW CAN OUR PORTS BE DEFENDED?

"How can this array be made most effective? Shall the artillery be afloat or ashore? Shall it be operated from forts or from vessels of war?

"The answers to these questions will bear a little enlargement. A harbor fleet, if as powerful as that of the enemy, would be expected to make, and doubtless would make, a good defense. Every one at all familiar with the history of our navy and its achievements will cheerfully concede that point. At best, however, in such a case, the chances of victory would be only equal to those of defeat, and it would seem to be very unwise to rest the security of important points upon any such contingency. But although our chances of victory would be quite equal to those of the enemy, the risks taken and the consequences to ensue from failure would be largely unequal, for while the enemy could lose nothing but his fleet, we could lose not only our fleet, but the much more valuable object that fleet was designed to protect. Where interests of great magnitude are at stake, ordinary prudence suggests that as little as possible should be left to the caprices of chance.

"To insure a perfect naval defense, therefore, the protecting fleet should be more powerful than the enemy's.

"Having determined what the naval strength shall be for the defense of our most important and valuable locality, it would be necessary to maintain an equal force at each and every other point deemed worthy of protection at all. Should we do otherwise, and assign smaller fleets to the smaller places, in proportion to their importance or value, an enemy arriving on our coast might, and if governed by wise and prudent counsels probably would, elect to defer his attempt upon our most valuable and therefore our best defended points, and direct his operations towards capturing or destroying in detail our smaller fleets, as well as the objects to whose defense they had been assigned. And, finally, after having accomplished this work at his own time and pleasure, he might, when confronted by an equal or superior force at our strong positions, decline battle altogether, and direct his efforts against our commerce upon the high seas, a commerce left entirely at his mercy by the policy which keeps the navy in port for home defense. The enemy having left his own ports well defended by fortifications—a condition substantially true of all great maritime powers except the United States—would be free to adopt this course."

ARE WE ABLE TO SEEK THE ENEMY ON THE OCEAN?

"If it be contended that a proper naval defense can be made by seeking the enemy upon the ocean, or by shutting him up in his own ports—thus leaving our coast entirely defenseless—the answer is, that such an assumption is not only at variance with all the lessons of history, but is in itself intrinsically illogical and weak. The power to escape from or evade an enemy upon the high seas, or break through a blockade, never very difficult of achievement, especially at night, even in the old time of sailing vessels, has been rendered comparatively easy and certain by the introduction of steam. The chances of success are indeed in a direct ratio with the speed attainable, admitting the speed of both parties to be the same, for the advantage in all such endeavors belongs to the party which takes the initiative. The history of ocean conflicts and cruises, of blockade-running and privateering, bears ample affirmative testimony on this point.

"Moreover, under this method of defense, the weight of advantage would be with the enemy, and the weight of risks with us. Being equipped and embarked for a naval attack upon our coast, he could scarcely wish to encounter our fleet, constituting the only defense of that coast, under circumstances of brighter promise to himself than those offering upon the broad ocean, for he could then either engage us in battle or withdraw under cover of night; and should he elect to withdraw, which would be the prudent course if inferior to us in strength, he could, at his option, either retire to his own fortified ports, pursue and destroy our commerce, or make a sudden descent upon our unprotected coast, as might suit his purpose best.

"If he adopt the last-named course, pursuing the original object of the expedition, he could even venture, for this purpose, to subdivide his fleet into small detachments, being certain of success at all points, because certain of finding our harbors unprotected by suitable fortifications, and our fleets absent upon the high seas.

"It would seem, therefore, that a cruising force, even if much more powerful than the enemy's, cannot be wisely relied upon for the defense of an extended seaboard.

A HINT THAT THE NATION SHOULD HEED.

"Not knowing where the enemy intends to strike, it would be necessary to be prepared for him at all points. If twelve armored vessels, properly equipped with torpedoes, be assumed as the limit of his offensive power, we must maintain more than a dozen fleets, each more powerful than the enemy's twelve vessels, in order to defend even a portion of our most populous cities and towns, and our most valuable depots and naval establishments. And even upon this broad and costly basis, nearly one-half of our harbors for armored vessels, and more than one-half of our entire Atlantic and Gulf coasts, would be left entirely defenseless.

"No estimate of the cost of such a method of defense will be made. Some idea of it may be gained from the fact that the single attacking fleet, if composed of the twelve British armored cruisers drawing twenty-six feet and less, will have originally cost about $18,000,000 for hulls and machinery alone, exclusive of armament and outfit." (See Report of Chief Engineer J. W. King, U. S. N.)

Dr. J. H. McLEAN'S IMPREGNABLE IRON FORTRESSES, MAGNETIC TORPEDOES, AND BREECH-LOADING GUNS, EXACTLY THE THING WANTED.

"The great cost of a defense by naval means, even in the first outlay for new vessels, excludes it from more than a moment's consideration, except for those points where adequate security cannot be obtained by a cheaper method. This objection becomes still more emphatic if we take into account the perishable nature of ships of war, and the constant and growing expense of preservation, repairs and renewals necessary to keep pace with the progress of the age. Notwithstanding its excessive cost, however, it is necessary to resort to this method of defense when the channels of approach to bays, sounds, and other partially land-locked waters are too wide to be effectively covered by land batteries. In such case, fortunately of rare occurrence on our coast, protection by floating means is indispensable if we would withhold these waters from use and occupation by the enemy. Long Island Sound, and Delaware and Chesapeake bays would have to be relinquished to a naval adversary, unless held by naval means. Fortifications at suitable points, however, even in these isolated cases, are necessary auxiliaries to the defense by a fleet in affording safe refuge under their guns for our mercantile marine, and points of rendezvous for our vessels of war in case of disaster, or while assembling before taking the offensive. But in nearly every case the channels leading to good harbors, safe anchorage, to cities, large towns and important establishments, are sufficiently restricted in width to be effectively defended by shore batteries and their accessories.

"Therefore, the important question is, can our main reliance against a naval attack be upon permanent fortifications aided by torpedoes?"

THE QUESTION ANSWERED.

As Gen. GILLMORE leaves the question with which he closes his valuable article unanswered, and apparently expects the country at large to answer it for him, Dr. J. H. McLEAN, as one of the representatives of that country, assumes the right to reply. Dr. McLEAN believes that if the government will construct a few of his permanent impregnable iron fortresses at the entrance of deep harbors, a few of his floating impregnable iron fortresses for the protection of shallow harbors, and twenty of his swift-sailing iron war ships, and arm these forts and ships with his Hercules Guns, our seacoast will be in danger from no source whatsoever. And the expense will not be worth considering, the more especially as the money would be directly disbursed among our own people, and the benefit thereof accrue to the whole nation. One such fort as Dr. J. H. McLEAN's Permanent Impregnable Iron Fortress, upon the site of Sumter, would have nipped the rebellion in the bud, and saved the nation three thousand millions of dollars and half a million lives. Ten such forts around Paris would have frustrated Germany, in 1871, and saved France thousands of millions, and spared her the most wretched humiliation it has ever been her lot to endure. One such fortress at Plevna would have made the Berlin Treaty unnecessary. Will the United States be wise in time, and by spending a few millions avoid the forced expense of thousands of millions?

MORE TESTIMONY AS TO THE DEFENSELESS CONDITION OF THE UNITED STATES.

The Hon. S. S. Cox, a member of Congress from the State of New York, in a recent speech before Congress, most eloquently depicted the defenseless condition of the coast and harbors of the United States. The following extracts from this speech will, no doubt, be read with much interest:

THE SPANISH NAVY SUPERIOR TO OUR OWN.

"The Spanish navy is much superior to ours in the number of vessels and their grade. It is made up of 148 vessels of all classes, and 809 guns, mostly rifles, heavy Rodman smooth-bores. Six of these ships are first-class iron clad frigates, and seven others are of the second class of armored ships.

"In our own navy, according to the report of the Secretary, we have eighty-one ships of all classes; and to this number is to be added four monitors and eight tugs, which can be fitted for cruisers or torpedo-boats, making a total of ninety-three vessels that could in time be fitted for service.

"We have not a sea-going iron clad in our navy. Monitors cannot remain at sea, even if they could be kept afloat in all weather; they cannot carry a supply of fuel for more than a few days, and do not carry sail. Their turret ports are so near the water that in rough weather they could not be opened; and, more than all, an 8-inch rifle at sixty yards can riddle their turret plating in half an hour."

OUR POVERTY IN EFFECTIVE GUNS.

"The piercing power of an 8-inch rifle is, theoretically, nine and eight-tenths inches at 500 yards, and nine and five-tenths at 1,000 yards. A target of 11-inch laminated plates is equal in resistance to six inches of solid iron platings. Our monitors are covered with eleven inches of plates, each of one inch thick, laid one over another, and at short range could not resist the 8-inch rifle of the Spanish navy, or any other, and would be destroyed by a gun of larger calibre at long range.

"Our one large rifle ($12\frac{1}{4}$-inch), now at Sandy Hook, cost about \$28,000. This gun has proved the equal, if not the superior, of any gun of foreign manufacture of equal calibre. It throws a shot weighing from six hundred to seven hundred pounds. See Report of Chief of Ordnance for 1878, in which, for results, the American gun is pronounced 'decidedly' superior to the Krupp and Italian guns, which use heavier charges than are required for ours to do the same work that they do."

IMMINENT DANGERS THAT THREATEN US.

"Herr Krupp, in response to a proposal from our officers to give a price for a 12-inch rifle, offered to manufacture and place on board ship for transportation a 12-inch rifle for the sum of $50,000 in gold, the conditions being that the gun should be tested under his own supervision. This is nearly double the cost of an American cast-iron gun of superior capacity and, as experience proves, equally safe and effective.

"Because we have escaped the penalties of our indifference so many years is no guarantee of such good fortune in the future. The property owners of New York, Boston, Philadelphia and Baltimore, and the coast cities generally, North and South, will hold somebody responsible for this perilous condition when the situation is thoroughly understood.

"Economy, based upon the idea that we can afford to postpone the work of suitably equipping our fortifications until a crisis arises, may prove a delusion, and of course will if we postpone action long enough.

"If a foreign power desire to bring on a war with us, for any purpose whatever, the fact that we are helpless and unprepared will stimulate the motive to hunt for a pretext."

WE PRESENT A PITIABLE SPECTACLE TO THE WORLD.

"A government based upon the will of 50,000,000 of people, rich, prosperous and abounding in resources, without the common means of defense of its honor and interests, presents a sorry spectacle to the world.

"Of course, Mr. Speaker, a member of this House of my economic notions yesterday expressed, both as to domestic frugality and foreign trade—loving and believing in the persuasive influences of free intercourse and reciprocal advantages—would naturally be disinclined to vote inordinate outlays for harbor defenses. He would prefer the cheap defense of fair customs duties and enlarged liberalities; but the millennium which ushers in his idealities has not yet begun to dawn, and he must consider contingencies of ominous aspect.

"Am I told that there is no danger of a breaking out of hostilities with other countries, and therefore no need of making appropriations for the armament of our forts? The time has not yet come for the lion and the lamb to lie down together; the ploughshare and pruning-hook are liable at any time to be converted into the bayonet and sword. The history of recent wars in Europe, Asia and Africa is a lesson of warning to us. Our increasing trade and growing relations with other countries admonish us to be ready at least for defense, if not for aggression."

OUR RELATIONS WITH SPAIN CRITICAL.

"Think of our critical relations with Spain! How often in late years have we been on the verge of conflict with Spain? Her present commercial relations with us are a perpetual menace. Her tariff so discriminates against this country that it is almost robbery. When we consider our exports and imports to Cuba alone, the discrimination against us is so marked an evidence of selfishness and enmity that it is almost a *casus belli*. For five years, from 1872 to 1876, we bought of Cuba on an average each year goods to the value of $71,364,327, while we sold but $15,466,139. This leaves the enormous balance against us of $55,898,188. During these years we purchased of Cuba to the amount of $356,821,638, while Cuba only bought in all $77,330,690, leaving a trade balance against us of $279,490,940. During the past twenty years Cuban exports to the United States have been increased at least 100 per cent. over our exports to Cuba, which have remained stationary. We have been Spain's best customer, especially in sugars. Yet how shabbily and meanly are we treated by her. The Spanish tariff favors her own vessels to such an extent as to deny to us advantages given other countries. Here is a statement of this rank injustice:

"A barrel of flour of Spanish production imported in a Spanish vessel would pay a duty of $2.25.

"The same flour imported in a foreign vessel would pay $4.50.

"A barrel of flour of foreign production imported in a Spanish vessel from any country, except the United States, would pay $4.69½.

"The same flour imported in a foreign vessel would pay $5.51.

"The discrimination against the United States can be realized when it is understood that a barrel of flour imported thence direct, either in a Spanish or foreign vessel, would have to pay the last-named duty, while, if it were sent to Canada and shipped from there, it would be subject only to the third class, or $4.69½, if shipped under the Spanish flag. Or, in other words, flour shipped direct from the United States, even in a Spanish vessel, would pay 40 per cent. more than Canadian flour, or the same flour shipped by way of Canada, in a similar vessel."

WE ARE AT THE MERCY OF SPAIN'S BIG GUNS.

"Do you say that this kind of tariff will be ameliorated? Never, while we are at the mercy of Spain's 800 rifled guns, her six first class iron-clads and her armored ships; never, while the city of New York can be placed under these guns and exactions made by the hundred millions.

"Is it not, therefore, wise and prudent to prepare, even by so small an appropriation, for the armament of our fortifications, that we may back our negotiations by proper force and make our country respected for its position as a power on the earth?"

IN TIMES OF PEACE PREPARE FOR WAR.

The true art of war consists as much in being always well prepared as in the artful prosecution of war after war has begun, and to have all the preparation for the defense of a nation to make after the attack begins, is exceedingly poor economy. One hundred millions of dollars, properly expended now in the building of Dr. J. H. McLean's impregnable fortresses and swift iron ships, and arming them with his wonderful peace-makers, will insure greater security to the nation than a thousand millions spent in temporary expedients and costly armaments after a war has been declared against us.

ADDITIONAL STARTLING EVIDENCE.
OUR COUNTRY PRACTICALLY WITHOUT A FORCE ON THE OCEAN.

So conspicuous has the weakness of our country become in the face of the gigantic armaments of other nations, that the people of the whole country are earnestly discussing the matter, and letters are pouring into Congress calling attention to the peril we are in. This stirring up of our public servants has resulted in a startling report made by the House Committee on Naval Affairs, from which the following extracts are made:

"Here are forty-eight vessels and no more, belonging to the navy to-day, capable of firing a gun, and of these, five are old, obsolete sailing vessels. If to these we were to add the eleven steam vessels repairing or awaiting repairs, the six iron clads repairing and awaiting repairs, the three steam vessels in ordinary, and the one unfinished second rate steam vessel, and assume that they can all be made fit for duty, the whole navy of the United States would at any one time number only sixty-nine vessels capable of carrying guns and doing naval duty. Such an assumption, however, will not be made by men of ordinary judgment. This is the whole of the navy of the United States, so far as it relates to fighting vessels. The fact may be disagreeable to contemplate and humiliating to American pride. In presenting it, however, we do but discharge a duty we owe to the House and to the people. The remedy and responsibility are not with the committee."

NOTHING BUT OLD-FASHIONED SMOOTH BORES.

"But we are weak in guns as well as in ships. We have less than two hundred and fifty guns afloat in our entire navy, and of these less than forty are rifled, a few eight-inch, a few 100-pounders and a few 60-pounders. All the rest are antiquated smooth bore."

The committee particularly point out that we have not one single rifled gun upon any of our iron clads, while every other power of even third rate importance is greatly our superior in weight, calibre and modern style of guns.

WHAT IS IMPERATIVELY NEEDED.

We want a navy capable of protecting our commerce on all seas, of defending our own borders from invasion, and of destroying the commerce and sea-going cruisers of any nation which may make war upon us. To do the first we should put our iron clad fleet in condition of the greatest efficiency, and should develop the torpedo system to its fullest extent. With our iron clad fleet in condition for coast and harbor defense, and our torpedo system perfected, 45,000,000 of Americans may defy all danger of foreign invasion. But we should be able not only to meet and beat off an invader from our shore, but also to extort from an enemy terms of honorable peace by aggressive war upon the high seas. The late war has taught us how much harm a few fast ships, gallantly commanded, can do upon the high seas, and the lesson should not be lost upon us. In the opinion of the committee the time has arrived when it is a national duty to begin the construction of a new navy. In any future wars with European nations we must fight upon the sea or nowhere. The committee do not recommend the expenditure of large sums with a view of perfecting such a navy this year or the next, but to commence the construction of three or four vessels a year, and to keep constantly employed a regular force of skilled employees; to employ the best skill in naval architecture, in engineering and gunnery, and to settle upon the best system and methods.

THE WHOLE GENIUS OF THE COUNTRY INVOKED.

The bill, which this committee recommends for passage, authorizes the Secretary of the navy to accept models, plans, &c., for ships, forts and guns from all sources, and to determine what sum shall be paid for the same. If, therefore, the authorities will honestly and impartially avail themselves of the privileges conferred by this bill it may be taken for assured that our country will not long be permitted to remain in her present defenseless condition.

LET THE UNITED STATES SPEND THREE HUNDRED MILLIONS IN THE NEXT FIVE YEARS

Among our own mechanics and working men. It will do the country good, first, by reason of the money thus released from the bars and bolts of the treasury and put into circulation among the people; and, secondly, because it will enable the United States to put herself into such a condition for defense and offense as will, at least, win for her the respect of her neighbors.

NO COUNTRY CAN AFFORD THIS OUTLAY SO WELL AS THE UNITED STATES CAN,

And yet in the face of this fact we behold even much poorer countries spending sums for ships, forts and big guns much greater than that which is named above. If the government is wise and will build no forts that are not positively impregnable, no ships except swift fighting ships, and then rely largely upon torpedoes to sink iron clads, no money will be wasted. Every inch of armor added to the already ponderous plating now burdening the war vessels of European powers is replied to by increased weight of attacking metal, and no armor exists to-day, upon any vessel afloat, that can positively be said to be impregnable. The effort to make ships impregnable must be abandoned, and swiftness and lightness be sought instead, while a radical change in the models will reduce the liability of damage from either shot or torpedoes.

Dr. J. H. McLEAN'S WONDERFUL HYDROPHONE.

As a fitting coronal to his other magnificent achievements, Dr. J. H. McLean has invented and partially perfected an instrument which may properly be termed a hydrophone. It is to be made fast to the bows of ships in the water, and will communicate instantly and distinctly all of the sounds of the sea. The roar of breakers, the splash of an oar, the blowing sound of a whale or grunt of a porpoise, the grinding noise of an iceberg, the splash of waves upon a beach, the noise of an approaching vessel, in fact, all sounds are gathered up by this wonderful mechanism and accurately conveyed to the ear of the man at the wheel.

The importance of such an invention can scarcely be measured. How many valuable lives and costly steamers might have been saved from icebergs, collision and breakers in the fogs off New Foundland had such a mechanism been attached to them? Surely, the world will have reason to bless the day that Dr. James Henry McLean first saw the light.

WHAT IS KNOWN ABOUT GUNS.

Despite the fact that considerable progress has been made in the construction of large cannon prior to 1860, the errors and prejudices which were common among military men respecting guns, have been largely adhered to and handed down by them from volume to volume, in the books which they have either compiled or written.

In discussing the proper shape for cannon, one military writer, only a few years since, insisted that the swell at the muzzle must not be abandoned, lest the *ball should split the muzzle*. The following is a fair illustration of what that writer declared was a perfect cannon in every respect, and more than half the guns now in use in all nations are no whit better than this old smooth bore.

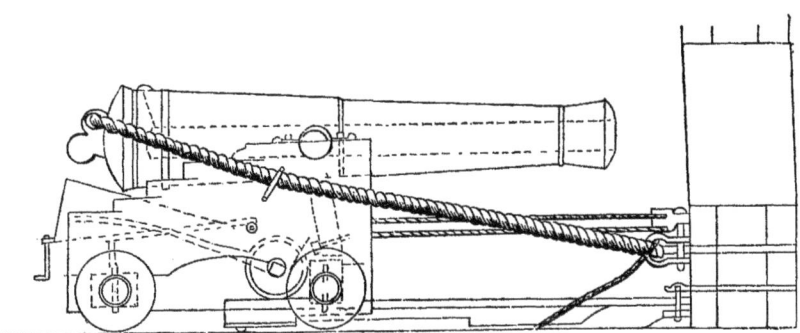

A Perfect Cannon, according to some Military Writers.

Men who have faith in the kind of gun shown above do not regard improved arms with any favor, and such men are more numerous in army and navy circles than will at first be believed. Dr. J. H. McLean is essentially a man of the people. He recognizes this as a people's world and government, and knows that if the people are satisfied that anything in use in either the army or navy of this country, is inferior to similar things offered by progressive men, the inferior thing is doomed and must go to the wall in time, despite the opinion of military men; therefore, he has chosen this method of bringing his arms into popular notice, before he submits them to the decision of any government. He wants the people to read and judge for themselves; and to show them how little is really known about guns, even by the men who make it their sole business to use them and write about them, he has caused all writers upon guns to be carefully read, and here presents the different conclusions arrived at by different writers, along with the varied and, in some cases, amusing reasons some of them give for their conclusions.

A HODGE PODGE OF OPINIONS.

Of cast iron guns Gen. GIBBONS says, on page 76 of his manual:

"Iron has no elasticity, and less tenacity than bronze, but losing gradually its cohesion, finally bursts at the breech suddenly, and without any external indication of the danger."

Lieutenant PARROTT, whose guns were so extensively used in the war of the Rebellion in this country, 1861-4, is quite of a contrary opinion respecting cast iron guns. His guns were all cast iron with a wrought iron re-inforce shrunk on around the breech, to strengthen that part of the gun where the greatest energy was developed in firing it. But his guns were exceedingly unfortunate, and had finally to be given up by the government as too dangerous to the men who worked them, to be longer retained. Their chief recommendation was their exceeding cheapness. Comparative costs will appear as follows: PARROTT gun, 10-inch bore, cost $4,500; ARMSTRONG, 10-inch, $9,000; KRUPP, 10-inch, $55,000; BLAKELEY, 10-inch, $17,500; WHITWORTH, 10-inch, $16,500. It will be seen that guns cannot be made for nothing. A BLAKELEY 12-inch costs $35,000, and a KRUPP 100 ton gun, throwing a shot about 16 inches in diameter and 1500 lbs. in weight, costs $125,000. The following illustrations will show the make of some of the prominent guns mentioned:

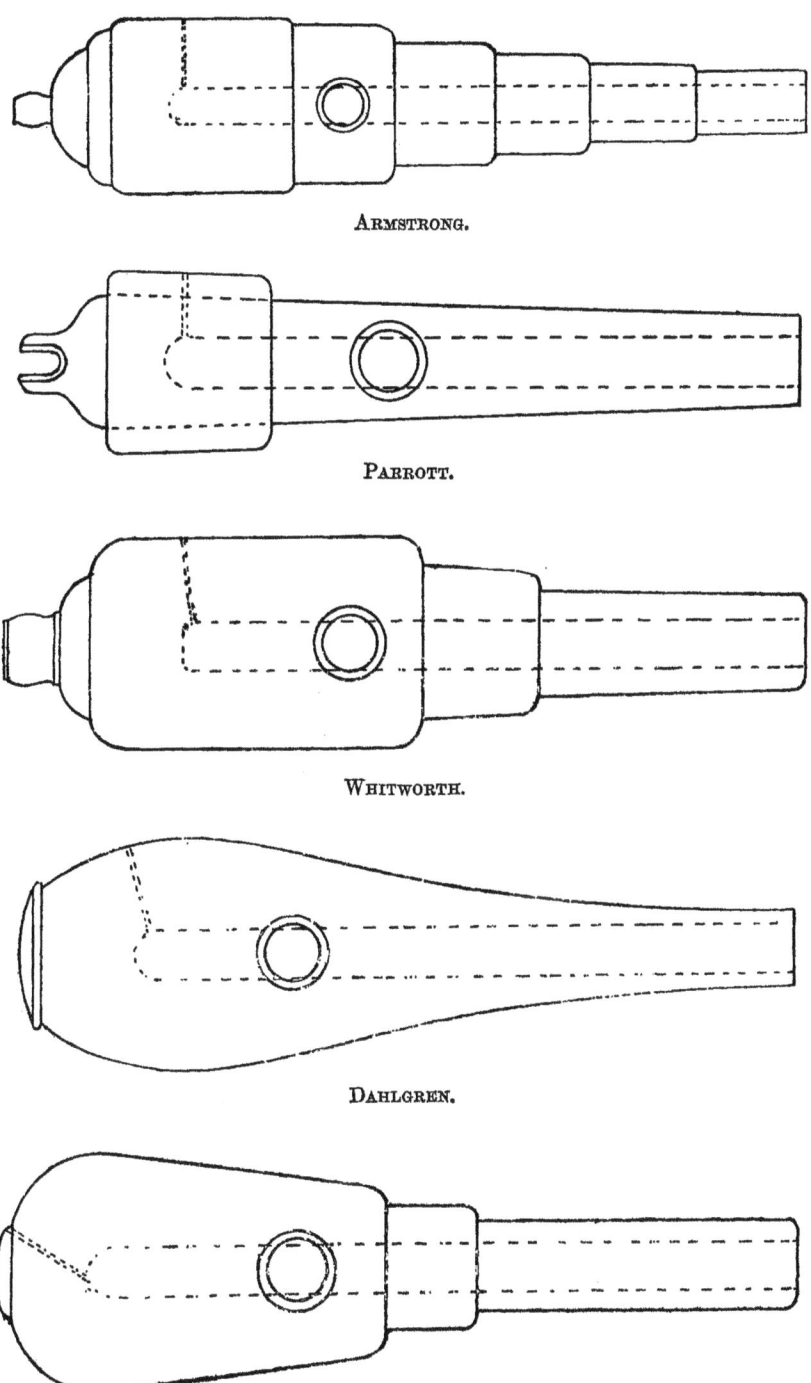

ARMSTRONG.

PARROTT.

WHITWORTH.

DAHLGREN.

BLAKELEY.

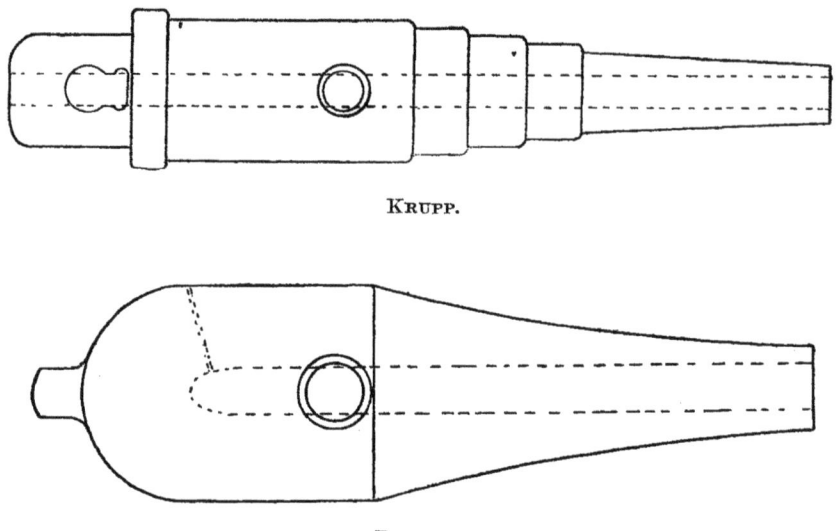

KRUPP.

RODMAN.

Of the 40 PARROTT guns used on Morris Island by Gen. GILLMORE, in his operations against Sumter, 29 of them burst, and in endeavoring to account for this extraordinary mortality of his guns, the inventor declares "*it must have been the sand that did it!*" The consumption of cannon in the siege of Sebastopol was not much less than on Morris Island, for Maj. DELAFIELD of the U. S. A., who was one of a Commission sent by the U. S. Government to report on that memorable struggle, says, on page 40:

"In the siege of Sebastopol, there were mounted and used in the English trenches alone, *nine hundred and eleven cannon*, and when the siege was over, only 250 of these were fit for further service."

GEN. SIMPSON'S IDEA OF WHY GUNS BURST; CAST IRON GUNS IN PARTICULAR.

On pages 97 and 98, Gen. SIMPSON, in his book on military matters, remarks:

"By the heat the gun is expanded; the expansion extends to the whole length of the bore, so that the whole gun becomes lengthened by the "end-on" strain of its expanded interior.

* * * "The upper side of the gun is relatively heated and expanded more than the lower side; and when the cross strain thus produced has bent the metal beyond the limit of its elastic recovery, the gun droops at the muzzle. * *

"The injuries which have been mentioned are common to all guns, but those of iron are subject to these effects in a less degree than bronze; iron guns, however, *have the inconvenience of bursting unexpectedly with small charges!*

"Formerly, when guns were subjected to great strain in the proof, they have been known to burst afterward with the service charge. This, very justly, has been charged to the effect of the heavy strain that the metal of the gun was subjected to at proof, a strain far greater than any that it would be called upon to endure in service. It is hence thought that many a good gun has been burst by subjecting it to an unfair strain in proof."

A SOMEWHAT CONTRADICTORY STATEMENT.

Military writers do not always take care to harmonize the opinions they express in their books about guns, with all of the facts they relate in other parts of their books about them. Gen. Simpson seems to afford the readiest illustration of what is here meant.

On page 109, Gen. Simpson says that old guns are extra hazardous; liable to fall to pieces at any time from the shock of a discharge. On page 115, he recites an experiment showing that a new gun burst at the 72d round, while one of similar calibre and metal, that had been in service eight years, stood a test of 2,582 rounds, and *was still sound.*

THE AVERAGE LIFE OF GUNS.

Gen. Simpson, on page 100, says, respecting the life-time of guns as they were at the time he wrote of them:

"The life-time of a gun is generally estimated at from one thousand to twelve hundred rounds, with service charge and a single projectile. Experience, however, proves that it is not only the great number of rounds fired which strains and destroys a gun, but that much influence is exerted by the high elevation at which a gun is fired in order to obtain range.

"A gun which, at 6° elevation, could stand without a strain two hundred rounds, would be likely, at an elevation of 30°, to burst before 50 rounds were fired. The explanation seems sufficiently simple:

"A gun fired at 6° elevation, recoils as the projectile is projected forward in proportion to its relative weight and friction; but when brought up to an elevation of 30°, the gun is entirely out of the horizontal, and the force is exerted downward, and the gun impinges on the solid earth, the deck of the ship or the carriage, and the shock is communicated to the sides of the gun."

THE SHORT-LIVED WOOLWICH GUNS.

Of the enduring qualities of the "Woolwich Infants," as our English cousins affectionately style them, the General does not seem to entertain a very favorable opinion, for he declares as follows:

"The life of a Woolwich gun is less than 400 rounds. A parliamentary report to April, 1866, shows that 60 per cent. of these guns were either burst or rendered unserviceable by an average of 210 rounds."

He proceeds to show why the Woolwich system of building "coiled guns" is defective:

"The heavy discharge of powder *heats and expands the inner tube* to a great degree, before the outer rings, which have no homogeneous connection with the inner, *are sufficiently heated to expand and give the inner tube room;* consequently the particles of the contiguous surfaces of these tubes are so compressed that when the firing has ceased, and the temperature of the gun returns to its normal state, the outer cylinders or rings *having had their particles compressed*, do not shrink sufficiently to bear upon the inner tube, which, at a subsequent firing, has to sustain the entire force of the explosion, until it heats and expands so as to get the support of the coils surrounding it. The seam between these coils widens as time wears on, and it is not uncommon to see a gun that has only been fired 40 or 50 times in such a state that the blade of a penknife might be inserted between the coils."

GENERAL UNCERTAINTY OF ALL CAST GUNS OF LARGE CALIBRE.

On page 84, Gen. SIMPSON says:

"The exterior, of course, cools first; and successive layers become solidified and contract until the center is reached, the particles of liquid metal being drawn out toward the cooling surface.

"The tendency of this is to produce a state of internal tension in the molecules of the metal, tearing away the external portions from the internal nucleus, and producing along the axis a line of weakness, where the metal is soft, porous, and with coarse and separated crystals, leaving, in spite of the constant feed of liquid metal through the dead-head, actual cavities in the centre of the castings.

"Fortunately, in pieces of artillery, this portion is nearly all bored out; but where the boring does not extend *well back to the exterior of the breech, a portion of this soft, spongy mass remains, forming the bottom of the bore.*"

PROFESSOR MALLET ILLUSTRATES WHY CAST GUNS GO TO PIECES SO UNEXPECTEDLY.

Referring to the arrangement of the crystals of metals in cooling, Mr. MALLET says:

"It is a law of the molecular aggregation of *crystalline solids* that, when their particles consolidate under the influence of heat in motion, their crystals arrange and group themselves, with their principal axes, in lines perpendicular to the cooling or heating surfaces of the solid, that is, in the lines of direction of the heat wave in motion, which is the direction of least pressure within the mass; and this is true, whether in the case of heat passing from a previously fused solid in the act of cooling and crystallizing on consolidation, or of a solid not having a crystalline structure, but capable of assuming one upon its temperature being sufficiently raised by heat applied to its external surfaces, and so passing into it.

"Any one who has ever remarked upon the formation and melting of ice will have seen the same principles exemplified on a grander scale. The little sharp crystals, as they form, are all lying flat upon the surface of the water; when, in the spring, the ice becomes rotten from the heat it has absorbed from the water beneath and the air on top, these crystals will all be found arranged vertically, and are easily pushed through by the weight of the foot or a stick. Large floating cakes of ice have been known to disappear on being struck by a vessel, or on striking the shore, sometimes called, though erroneously, the 'sinking of the ice.' The shock destroys the little cohesion remaining between the crystals, and the whole mass falls apart.

"Cast iron is one of the substances which, in cooling, obeys more or less perfectly this law."

SOME AMUSING OPINIONS ABOUT GUNS—RIFLED CANNON AND BREECH-LOADING ARMS CONDEMNED.

In view of the progress made towards providing the armies and navies of the world with really effective weapons, the following *very military* opinions about *proposed* improvements in guns will be highly interesting reading:

On page 389, Gen. SIMPSON says of the impertinent attempt to rifle cannon:

"Many attempts have been made to apply the rifle principle to guns of large calibre, but up to the present time the success of inventors in this line has not been such as to warrant the introduction of rifled cannon to any great amount in the batteries of ships; although for light pieces for the field and boat howitzers, the application of the system seems to be approved of to a considerable extent. The *importance of the question is much enhanced by the fact that the moment a successful plan is discovered, the problem of percussion shells is solved!*"

On the same subject Major DELAFIELD very dubiously remarks, on page 9 of his report to the U. S. Government, on the Crimean War:

"An attempt is being made by several of the European powers to adopt the rifle principle to artillery, and has been so far successful as to cause its introduction into the armament of part of the expedition against Cronstadt in 1856."

Major DELAFIELD majestically reserves his opinion as to the success of this daring innovation upon the rights of the military. Still he is pretty well satisfied that there is room for *some* improvement in the arms used, for in the following article he gracefully

BIDS FAREWELL TO THE OLD-FASHIONED MUSKET,

with its smooth bore, its ringing ramrod, its flint lock, and ungainly stock, and admits that, perhaps, a good rifled shoulder gun, with a percussion lock, is the better arm of the two. On page 21 he says:

"The introduction of the long gun to fire shells horizontally, both for land and sea service, with a tendency to increase the calibre, and of the rifle, with various modifications for all small arms, may now be considered as the settled policy and practice of all the military powers of Europe.

"The belief in the superiority of these two principles was so well established, that all the powers engaged in the late great contest (the Crimean War), as well as the neighboring neutrals, *were driven to follow* each other in their introduction as fast as their manufacture would permit. *For want of time to prepare the most approved weapons, modifications of the existing arms in the arsenals and depots* were resorted to by the different powers." * * * * Page 6. "The rifle is now the common arm for the infantry of *all* the European armies. The smooth bore is no longer made for military service. Its use may be considered as confined to old patterns that circumstances have not yet permitted to be altered. The percussion lock is universal."

BUT HE DON'T WANT ANY BREECH-LOADING RIFLES IN HIS'N.

Maj. DELAFIELD, in favorably reporting upon changes in guns of so radical a nature as the above, undoubtedly felt that he was making all the concession to the impudent and tiresome demands of progress, that any man of his education and respectable prejudices could consistently make, so he intrenched at once, and thus, with "faint praise," everlastingly squelches the German "needle-gun":

"Prussia alone, of all continental powers, has adopted a breech-loading musket, for her armies, called the needle-gun; and although in use in her army for many years past, and well known in all its details, no other nation has been willing to follow her example.

"Celerity and rapidity of fire are the main points aimed at by the many inventors and advocates of this modification of the musket. We know, that with the present weapons, hundreds of rounds of ammunition are fired without producing any effect, and probably not one shot in a thousand rounds issued to the soldier ever does execution. The contest in the Crimea, as well as all previous wars, establishes this waste of cartridges. It is steadiness and aim at the object, by the soldier, that must be secured; a principle at variance with rapidity and celerity."

WHAT OTHER UNITED STATES OFFICERS SAID OF THE NEEDLE-GUN A LITTLE LATER.

The United States sent a Military Commission to attend the Paris Exposition of 1868, and to make a full and careful report upon all improvements which they might note in arms and other things relating to the defense of a great nation. The victories of the Prussians over the Austrians had become history, and the needle-gun appeared in a light quite different from the one it was viewed in by Maj. DELAFIELD. The Commissioners say of it:

"The success of this weapon in the late war, was due to the fact of its being a *breech-loader*, rather than to any virtue dependent on its construction, and any other *good* breech-loader would have had an equal advantage over the muzzle-loading gun with which the opposing army was furnished."

MORE RICHNESS! GEN. SIMPSON SAYS BREECH-LOADING GUNS NEVER CAN SUCCEED!

An English gentleman of acknowledged scientific attainments, published, in pamphlet form, a lengthy, very scientific and very elaborate article, establishing, beyond all doubt, the utter impossibility of sending messages through a submarine cable laid across the ocean. His pamphlet appeared just in time to secure the appearance in the public journals of the world, of choice extracts from it, along with the extraordinary news that the cable had proved an unqualified success. Some of the richest arguments of the learned gentleman were actually "cabled" from England to the New York papers. This gentleman's case is not the only illustration of the sudden overthrow of dogmatic assertion by the rush of progressive *facts*. Here is another. On page 418 of his book, Gen. SIMPSON thus sweepingly condemns breech-loaders in general, and breech-loading cannon in particular:

"In spite of the apparent success of breech-loading guns, *objections exist which go to prove* that the endeavor to produce breech-loading cannon is an effort to obtain uncalled for and superfluous facility in gunnery.

"What superior property can it possess over the solid gun?

"It cannot be safety; for when we consider the very limited number of explosions by which *the very best guns are destroyed*, it can scarcely be possible for a gun composed of many parts, to endure the intense vibrations to which large cannon are subjected. Vibration, if judiciously distributed, is the soul of endurance (?) but if injudiciously distributed, is certain to result in the destruction of the cannon. In structures composed necessarily of many joints, obstructions to the waves of vibration must occur; the different parts do not expand and vibrate equally, a kind of revulsion (?) is induced, part repels part (?) and destruction ensues as a natural consequence.

"Under *no* circumstances, therefore, can a breech-loading gun be as safe as a solid gun.

"The faculty of loading, and rapidity with which a breech-loading piece can be fired, are spoken of as advantages of great importance, but these amount to nothing, for the gun, after every discharge, must be relayed in order to obtain accuracy of aim, and it is the pointing of a gun, and not the loading, that consumes time.

"Again, the tendency of all guns to absorb the heat developed during the explosion, puts a limit to all extreme rapidity of fire. During the Russian war at Sveaborg, it was found necessary to allow an interval of 5 minutes between each discharge of a mortar, and yet the whole of them burst after an average of 120 shots."

MILITARY MEN WHO BELIEVE THE CONTRARY.

The Military Commission sent to Paris, before referred to, evidently became convinced that not only had breech-loading rifles become a vital necessity in the armament of a nation, but that breech-loading cannon might also be enumerated in the same category. On page 50, of their report to the government, they declare as follows:

"In regard to breech-loading cannon and other arms, whatever objections may be raised against them on account of their tendency to waste ammunition, it is plain that in future wars they will occupy an important place, *and the nation which neglects to adopt some good breech-loading gun for its armies will stand on a slippery basis.*"

THIS IS PRECISELY Dr. McLEAN'S OPINION.

The nation that fails to adopt those weapons of all kinds—cannon, shells, torpedoes and small arms—that will do the most rapid and effective work, "*stands on a slippery basis*" sure enough! In a campaign of but a few weeks duration the Prussians almost destroyed the entire Austrian army, because the Prussians were armed with a breech-loading rifle, while the dignified, highly respectable and loyally *conservative* military men of Austria had, in harmony with the opinions of our own SIMPSON and DELAFIELD, decided that "in spite of the *apparent* success of the breech-loader" it was an unmitigated humbug, and the old reliable muzzle-loader should be adhered to by the Royal Austrian Army. They were prepared to stand by this opinion to the death; and they did!

Had Gen. SIMPSON led an Austrian column into battle against the Prussians before he wrote the following, it is presumed page 113 of his book would have contained some other matter:

"When it is remembered that soldiers in action, even when well disciplined, expend from 10,000 to 30,000 cartridges for every man disabled, it becomes a self-evident fact that they fire too fast already, and that it is only adding to the evil to give them the means of firing four or five times as fast, by placing breech-loading guns in their hands."

That soldiers, armed with a muzzle-loading gun, *do* "fire too fast already," *is* a self-evident fact, as the General says, because they fire ineffectively. Stand up a line of men close together, shoulder touching shoulder, exposed to a storm of bullets, grape, cannon shot and shell, and that line of men, however well disciplined, will be nervous, because they know that seven-eighths of their time will be passed in *loading their guns.* Naturally, they will blaze away in haste, and without even properly leveling their pieces, as quick as the load is down; but now consider Dr. McLean's proposition for a moment:

DROP THE MEN DOWN BEHIND HIS IRON FORMS,

Give them one of his 128-shot magazine rifles, and let the officer in command issue strict orders to the men not to fire rapidly except when the enemy is charging their line or are fully exposed in dense masses. Does Gen. Simpson, or any other officer, suppose that it would then take 10,000 rounds of ammunition to disable one man? Preposterous! The men, lying behind their iron forms, would not feel nervous. On the contrary, they would feel *secure*, and would fire only when they felt sure of damaging the enemy.

METHODS OF CONSTRUCTING MANY OF THE CELEBRATED GUNS.

The Parrott gun is a cast iron cylinder, rifled and reinforced around the breech with a jacket of wrought iron, shrunk in.

The Armstrong gun is formed of separate cylinders, made of wrought iron coils, shrunk together, and arranged, as to thickness, so as to best resist the pressure of the charge.

The Blakeley gun has an inner tube made of low steel, and a second tube of high steel, shrunk on to the inner one. Then an outer jacket to which the trunnions are attached, also shrunk on.

The Woolwich guns have a solid steel core cast, and around this is shrunk the various layers of metal built of wrought iron coils. The steel core is then bored out to the required size.

The Whitworth gun has a central tube of steel. Over this another steel tube is shrunk, and around these two tubes hoops of steel are also shrunk and hammered on.

The Krupp gun is built up by shrinking hoops of steel over a central steel tube. In large calibres the layers of hoops are double.

The Rodman gun is of cast iron. It is cast around a hollow steel core supplied with flowing water, and thus the gun is cooled from the interior outward as well as from the exterior inward.

The Dr. J. H. McLean Hercules gun will be constructed quite differently from all those above described, and upon strictly practical and scientific principles. In the first place,

THE BARREL WILL BE FORMED OF THREE SEPARATE TUBES,

Of the best fluid-compressed steel, hammered to a proper thickness, upon a steel mandril. These three steel tubes will be then put into a lathe and turned so as to fit easily into each other, according to their respective diameters. They will not be shrunk together, but, as shown in the following diagrams, will be threaded at one end only, and simply pushed in and screwed together.

Now here is a fearful departure from the old beaten track of shrinking parts or layers of metal together, or forcing them together by hydrostatic pressure! Well, the truth is, Dr. J. H. McLean has found out that nearly all of the old fashioned ways of doing things are inferior ways, and he prefers to strike out an entirely new path of his own.

So, he will simply shove his three tubes together and screw them into each other at one end only.

Now when the gun barrel begins to heat, the metal begins to elongate, does it not? Very good! The molecules of metal directly around the flame of the powder, grow hottest and elongate quickest, and if the inside tube were screwed on at both ends, there would be a strain tending to bow the inner tube upward, because the outer or middle tube, not being as hot as the inner one, would not expand as rapidly. But if the tubes fit each other easily and are only screwed into each other at one end, then the inner tube, when it grows hot, can expand without any strain, then the middle one can also expand according to its measure of heat and the outer one do the same without ever straining the gun at all.

Professor Barlow, many years ago, proved to the satisfaction of the Institution of Civil Engineers, that the metal in a cylinder decreases in utility in

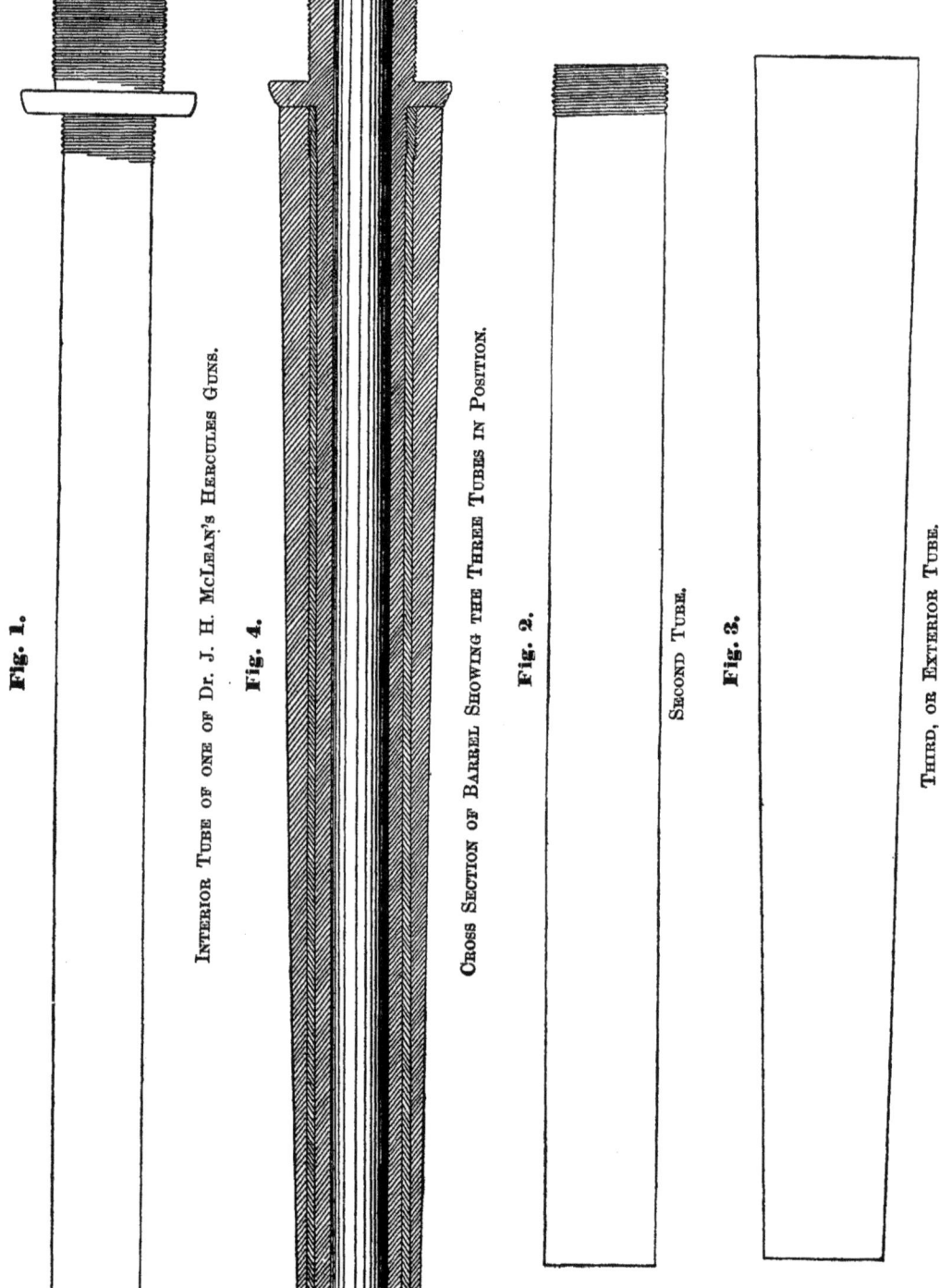

Fig. 1. Interior Tube of one of Dr. J. H. McLean's Hercules Guns.
Fig. 4. Cross Section of Barrel Showing the Three Tubes in Position.
Fig. 2. Second Tube.
Fig. 3. Third, or Exterior Tube.

proportion to the square of its distance from the center; that the outside of a gun of the form now used, is only one-ninth as useful as the inside, being three times as far from the center.

Agreeing perfectly with Prof. Barlow, Dr. J. H. McLean will apply the scientific fact stated above in the construction of his guns. He will construct the inner cylinder three times as thick as the outer one, and the middle one twice as thick as the outer one. Thus, the inner one might be three inches, the middle one two and the outer one one inch in thickness, because the one inch of exterior metal would have as much resisting power as would the three inches of interior metal, and when the exact amount of metal required to resist the strain to which the gun can be subjected is ascertained, the addition of more is unnecessary.

BUT THE GREATEST STRAIN ON THE HERCULES GUN

comes upon the slide, and into this slide, at every discharge, is thrust a fresh steel shell. Therefore the wearing, eating, rotting, shattering effects which a course of long continued firing has upon guns as now constructed, do not apply to Dr. J. H. McLean's guns at all, for that particular portion of the gun wherein the powder is burned, is renewed in his guns, with every discharge. Not only is this true, but his *recoil cushion* is another potent gun saver. In overcoming the inertia of a very large shot, the force exerted upon the gun by the confined gas is tremendous, and the gun, at every discharge, is weakened and less able to endure the next, and finally bursts. But when the Hercules guns are fired, the steel shell containing the powder darts backward upon the rubber recoil cushion, and the gas has room to expand while overcoming the inertia of the shot, thus very materially lessening the strain upon the gun and indefinitely prolonging its life.

The illustration on page 64, will afford the reader a very good idea of what one of Dr. J. H. McLean's 100-ton Hercules guns will look like when built and placed on board a swift iron ship, not an armored ship, but such an one as will be found fully described in another portion of this book. The illustration here shows the gun mounted upon its vertically moving pedestal, and those who will study it carefully, will acknowledge that it is the champion gun of the world.

A GOOD OLD GUN CROWDED OUT BY IMPERTINENT INVENTORS.

For a long time the brass guns of Turkey, on the Dardanelles and Bosphorus, have been known as the largest sea coast guns in use in any European works. They are 20 to 30 inches in diameter of bore, and are provided with stone shot, *have to be loaded on the outside of the fort*, and, having *no trunnions*, can only be fired with a fixed elevation, and mounted on a carriage or block that admits of no horizontal rotation.

Impertinent inventors like Dr. McLean, have finally succeeded in making it necessary to pull in these old fellows, and actually use the new fangled ordinance of an impudent, unbelieving age of progress. So mote it ever be.

A GREAT GUN MANUFACTURING CO. TO BE ESTABLISHED.

In order to carry on the business of manufacturing his great Peace-Makers, Dr. McLean intends to establish in the United States a company with a subscribed capital of $20,000,000, thus surpassing the great Krupp Company in Germany and the Armstrong Company in England. The natural resources of the United States are unequaled on the globe, and, in process of time, the comprehensiveness and cheapness of her transportation facilities, the low price of her raw material and of her food, the immunity of her people from burdensome taxation and from military service, the attractiveness of her free institutions, free schools and free land, *must make her the leading manufacturing and commercial nation of the world!* This statement cannot be successfully controverted, for, in addition to the overtopping inventive genius and mechanical expertness of our own people, thousands of the most skillful artizans of Europe annually seek a home in our great and glorious Republic. Thus, with every requisite at hand, it is impossible that we should not eventually lead all the nations of the earth in every form of industry and barter. At the present time there does not exist in the entire United States a single firm or corporation capable of producing in an economical and workmanlike manner one such gun as Dr. McLean's proposed 100-ton Hercules, and were the government desirous to build such guns it would be compelled to send the contract abroad.

Dr. J. H. McLEAN PROPOSES TO STOP ALL SUCH NONSENSE

by organizing a colossal company for the purpose of building his great Peace-Makers. Under this comprehensive term are included his surf-fighting ships, his impregnable fortresses, his iron forms, his magnetic torpedoes, his terrible shells and the entire range of his magazine arms, battery guns and monster breech-loading cannon. All persons who feel an interest in the establishment of such a company should address Dr. J. H. McLean at St. Louis, Mo. By reading the following article clipped from the *New York Sun* of May 4th, 1880, it will be seen that the great guns of Europe are not to be relied upon, and that it is high time America was furnishing a more reliable and perfect weapon to the world:

GUNS DANGEROUS TO FRIEND AND FOE.

"We have now the particulars concerning the bursting of the 100-ton gun at Spezia last month. This huge rifle, of the largest size yet constructed, was mounted in one of the turrets of the Italian Duilio, the most powerful iron clad in the world. Its fate is important because it teaches us anew the perils which attend the handling of the great modern guns of which so much was expected, and again shows them to be nothing more than experiments in ordnance.

"It is only a little over a year since a 38-ton gun on the English Thunderer burst during practice. This gun, which at that time was one of the most powerful in use, and had been constructed with infinite pains, was blown into fragments, and everybody in its vicinity was either killed or wounded, while much damage was done to the turret of the vessel. It was surmised that the gun had been doubly loaded through the carelessness of those handling it; but as that is an accident not unlikely to happen under the excitement of action, a gun of the same size was last winter tested at Woolwich with a double charge. Like the Thunderer gun, it was blown to pieces."

THE WOOLWICH SYSTEM DISTRUSTED.

"These experiences with the 38-ton gun cannot fail to throw doubt on all the guns manufactured after the system used in its construction, the one employed at Woolwich. It is a pretty severe strain on the nerves to fire one of these hugh rifles in a turret, even if the gunners have confidence in the weapon; but if they feel that every time they discharge it they take their lives in their hands, they can hardly be blamed if they are a good deal demoralized. It is plain that to make these huge rifles of the highest effectiveness in war, it must be demonstrated that they are no longer likely to be as dangerous to those who serve them as to those against whom they are directed."

DOUBTS ABOUT THE ARMSTRONG SYSTEM.

"While the bursting of the 38-ton guns has so lately brought suspicion on the Woolwich system of manufacture, after which a large share of the guns in the British navy are constructed, the bursting of the 100-ton gun on the Duilio now raises doubts of the soundness of the Armstrong system, the one on which it was built. Thus, of the small number of systems of heavy gun manufacture with which we are familiar—the Woolwich, the Armstrong, the Palliser, the Whitworth, and the Krupp—two have been brought under condemnation. And yet, with the difficulties of manufacture vastly increasing with the size of the gun, experimental rifles of 81 tons have been made after the Woolwich system, and drawings for guns on the same plan to weigh between 160 and 200 tons have been prepared. At the Elswick Works, where the Armstrong guns are made, rifles of 150 tons are to be constructed. Krupp, too, has a design for a breech-loader of 124 tons.

"The gun at Spezia burst on the first fire. It was loaded with 521 pounds of powder and a shot weighing 2,000 pounds; a charge intended to be used when the full power of the gun is to be called into play. It was not blown into fragments like the Thunderer's gun, but broke into two pieces. The whole of the muzzle, together with the trunnions, remained fixed to the carriage, while the rest of the gun was blown backward against the wall of the turret, doing much damage to the vessel, but destroying no lives."

A PERTINENT QUESTION.

"If these great guns, the fruits of the most consummate engineering skill, and the results of long and careful experiment, are liable to burst into many fragments, or to be blown apart during the comparatively cautious trials in time of peace, what will be their fate and the fate of those who handle them amid the haste of war?

"With their own weapons menacing the lives of the gunners and threatening the ship, and with torpedoes below its armored sides, ready to send the whole craft to the bottom, one of the huge iron clads upon which Europe is lavishing so much money would have reason to hesitate before it attempted the passage of a properly defended channel. Only here and there a gun may burst, but one such catastrophe destroys confidence in the whole number."

Take another look at the illustration of Dr. J. H. McLean's Hercules gun, and read a second time the description of the system upon which these splendid guns are to be constructed.

THE HERCULES GUN.

In attempting a thorough improvement in guns, it was deemed best to begin with those which have remained longest in their primitive condition, as it were. Cannon, as they are at present found in the armaments of all nations, are, as a rule, very little changed from the patterns a century old. They are simply tubes of metal, of variable length and variable diameters. The powder is inclosed in a bag and rammed in at the muzzle, shoving all the dirt and soot which may have escaped the hasty swabber ahead of it to choke the vent; the ball is rammed in on top of the powder, and that it may be sure to go down solid and not cause the gun to burst, it is made to fit the bore loosely, thus providing a heavy "windage" and consequent waste of powder energy. After the gun is thus slowly and laboriously charged, it is "touched off" with a coal, a hot iron, a priming quill, or some such primitive device, and again the swabbers and rammers "pitch in" to get the piece ready to fire again. Slowly and badly served as such guns necessarily are, they become dangerously hot, and the explosion of the bag of powder while being rammed home is not an uncommon occurrence, and many a poor swabber has been instantly torn to shreds in consequence.

When one wishes to improve an article of any kind, he naturally determines first the nature of the defects which he proposes to remedy. The present defects in heavy ordnance are many, and it is proposed that they shall be pointed out by experienced military men who have used and written about them.

BURSTING OF CANNON.

The bursting of guns in action is a calamity from every point of consideration.

First. The possible loss of valuable lives, occasioned by such bursting, must be considered.

Second. The loss of the service of the gun at a possibly critical moment.

Third. The loss of the gun considered as a piece of property.

Fourth. The possible disarrangement of the whole plan of attack.

Fifth. The sad demoralization of men connected with guns liable to burst.

In 1863, Maj.-Gen. GILLMORE, in command of Morris Island, had 30 Parrott guns in his batteries, and upon being directed to reduce Forts Sumter and Wagner by bombardment, sent to the War Department for several more of the Parrott guns, giving his reason therefore, on page 21 of his published report, as follows:

"As the endurance of the Parrott guns of heavy calibre was, at that time, a matter of some distrust and uncertainty, requisitions were sent forward for several more of them, which were promptly filled by the Ordnance Department."

The result of the bombardment showed that the distrust of the Parrotts was only too well founded, for in the two week's bombardment that ensued, 28 out of less than 40 guns in action, bursted.

What the casualties to the operators of the bursted pieces were is not told, but that they were severe is inferred from the statement made by an officer of one of the batteries, that the guns came to be so dreaded by officers and men alike, that slow matches were used in firing them, so as to enable the gunners to rush into the bomb proofs before the discharge occurred.

Gen. GILLMORE says: "What the service now imperatively demands is heavy artillery that will stand the average test of 1,000 rounds. The Parrotts did not stand the test of an average of 300 rounds."

Dr. J. H. McLean agrees to build guns that *will not burst.*

Dr. McLean guarantees his guns for 3,000 rounds, and farther guarantees that at the expiration of that trial they will be still "as good as new"—in perfect firing trim.

This is one of the most important features possessed by his peacemakers. They will inspire the confidence of the gunners, first because they cannot be bursted, and second because of their great rapidity of fire, no delay being necessitated by their heating.

Not long since one of the big ARMSTRONG guns of the English iron clad "Thunderer" burst and killed and maimed several men. The following is the official account telegraphed to the English Admiralty, by Vice-Admiral Sir G. PHIPPS HORNBY:

"ISMID, January 2, 1879.

"One 38-ton gun in the Thunderer burst this morning, killing Lieutenant Coker and Lieutenant Daniel, R. M. A.; George Fern, Isaac Grover and John Roche, petty officers; George H. Butland, William Monday and William Warn, leading seamen; Henry Bezzel, able seaman; and Thomas Bolton, corporal R. M. Gun burst just before trunnion, muzzle blowing overboard. The gun had been fired with battering charge, but when it burst was loaded only with full charge and empty shell. Mr. Jackson, boatswain, and 32 men wounded, 12 very badly. Turret is disabled, ship otherwise uninjured. I will report condition of the wounded to-morrow."

The true cause of the terrible disaster is unknown, but in naval circles at Portsmouth, it is supposed that the muzzle of the gun being depressed, the paper match which was used to keep the shot in its place became shrunken from the effects of the climate, and it thus slipped from the breech toward the muzzle. The compactness of the charge became disturbed, and, as a consequence, the force of the explosion flew to the weakest part, and hence the bursting of the gun.

THEY WOULD NOT BELIEVE IT.

The announcement that one of the 38-ton guns on board her Majesty's ship Thunderer had burst, was received at the Royal Arsenal at Woolwich with mingled consternation and incredulity. That one of the Woolwich guns, built up of tough wrought iron spirals, coil upon coil, had burst, passed belief. Such an accident had never occurred since the introduction of the Woolwich system, and in all the experiments in which guns of this character have been "proved to destruction," it has been found impossible to produce a sudden burst, the only effect, after 2,000 rounds, or 20 of the heaviest charges, being gradually to weaken and break up the gun, with ample warning even in the earliest stages of the process. It had become a fundamental principle in the Royal Gun factories, that, by fair means, it was not possible to burst one of its guns, and although experience has shown that it is the unlikely which happens, the officers of the department are of the same opinion still.

IT WAS A MUZZLE-LOADER, OF COURSE!

As this gun was a muzzle-loader, it had to be slanted downward to take in the shot, and the great weight of the shot made it necessary that it should be rammed home by powerful machinery. When this rammer was withdrawn, the gun was still slanted downward, and it is pretty sure the great shot slipped forward in the barrel, leaving a vacant space between the bag of powder and the shot. Such an accident cannot occur to the Dr. McLean's breech-loading Hercules gun, because the gun is either perfectly horizontal when loaded, or inclined to a greater or less upward angle. Besides this, the shot fits the barrel much too snugly to permit its slipping forward of its own weight. This would be the case even where the shot and the charge of powder form two separate packages, as is now universally the case in breech-loading cannon, but in Dr. McLean's Peace-Makers the powder and the bolt are both confined in a steel shell, and by this means a much greater security is attained.

NO SWABBERS WANTED FOR THE PEACE-MAKERS.

Though the ordinary breech-loading cannon may be quite rapidly fired without swabbing, it nevertheless gets so hot in a brief action as to render the thrusting of a bag of powder into the chamber dangerous, and therefore they must be allowed to cool off. But Dr. J. H. McLean's Peace-Makers can be fired with four times the rapidity of any other breech-loading ordnance, and it is immaterial how hot the barrel of the gun may get. The steel slide into which the cold steel shells are thrust, is always cool, and premature explosion is impossible. The gun needs no swabbing, no matter how protracted the action may be!

GEN. GILLMORE ON DEFECTS IN CANNON.

On page 99 of his report referred to above, Gen. Gillmore says:

"A safe and advantageous arrangement and distribution of the materials of a large gun, particularly of a rifled gun, to enable it to sustain the successive strains and shocks to which they will be subjected in firing, *is incompatible with the condition that the gun shall be composed of a single piece of homogeneous metal.*"

Bear in mind that all of the cannon proposed by Dr. J. H. McLean are to be composed of several parts. The barrel is always manufactured by itself, and for guns of the largest calibre this would be formed of three distinct steel cylinders.

Then there is the breech, the slide and the steel shell, all of which play a prominent part in making up an unburstable cannon.

On the same page Gen. Gillmore continues:

"In firing, the bore of the gun *rapidly receives a permanent enlargement within the limit of rupture.*

"The forces which act upon a gun tending to destroy it are due principally to the explosive force of the powder *and the expansion of the gun by heat.*"

The Dr. J. H. McLean arms are *all* supplied with steel shells, and consequently the chamber of the gun itself never becomes hot. Hence another and a chief reason why guns burst is met and overcome.

THE HERCULES GUN. 105

Brig.-Gen. TURNER, reporting to Gen. GILLMORE, on page 150, says:

"The 8-inch rifled guns were fired about once in seven minutes, but the 10-inch never faster than once in ten minutes. Even then the guns were washed out thoroughly at every twentieth round and allowed to cool, as they became quite hot after this number of rounds had been fired.

"The guns were thoroughly oiled every third shot, and all the projectiles were carefully greased."

AFRAID OF THEIR GUNS!

The reader will admit that once in seven minutes for an 8-inch gun, and once in ten minutes for a 10-inch gun is *rather slow firing!*

What occasioned these long intervals between one shot and another?

FEAR! That was it!

Fear that the guns would heat and burst!

Dr. J. H. McLEAN *will guarantee that his guns may be safely fired five times a minute all day!*

BURSTING OF THE SWAMP ANGEL!

Doubtless the entire reading world has heard of the "*Swamp Angel.*" This was an 8-inch Parrott gun erected by Gen. Gillmore's forces, on Morris Island, in 1863, to shell the city of Charleston, S. C. From the ship which transported it, it was hauled to its position with no little labor, and with still greater labor and expense an earthwork was thrown up for it.

Great things were expected of this gun. Telegrams of the shelling of Charleston by the great Swamp Angel, six miles away, were flashed all over the North. But suddenly these glowing accounts died away. The rebels did not evacuate Charleston. Nothing more was said about the Swamp Angel!

What was the matter?

It had burst on the 36th round! That was what was the matter.

But the country was not told of this at the time, nor of the bursting of the other twenty-eight Parrott guns.

WHAT THE SERVICE DEMANDS.

With these disasters in his mind, Gen. GILLMORE says, in his report, page 97:

"What the service demands is a gun strong enough to sustain the repeated shock of at least one thousand charges of powder, in as large quantities as can be burned with useful effect behind the projectile, and at any required elevation. The average duration of the Parrott guns was 210 shots."

EXACTLY! That is just what the service demands, and precisely what Dr. J. H. McLEAN has provided for the service. THE HERCULES GUN IS THAT VERY GUN! And more! It will do better than 1,000 charges, better than 3,000 charges! In fact it may be said to be comparatively *indestructible!*

THE DEFECT OF RECOIL.

Gen. SIMPSON, author of Ordnance and Naval Gunnery, says, on page 80:

"It is evident that in firing a gun, the bottom of the bore is re-acted upon by a force equal to that which drives before it the projectile and the unconsumed portion of the charge itself, for the inflammation of the charge is not instantaneous. We may, then, conclude that if the gun is of the same weight as the projectile, it will take up a motion in a contrary direction with a velocity proportionately greater, as the charge is heavier. The excess of velocity is due to the weight of the charge, the gases of which continue to react upon the bottom of the bore after the projectile has left the gun. The retrograde movement imparted to the gun by the effect of the charge is called the recoil, and should be kept in certain limits, that the service of the gun may be convenient. Now, we know in mechanics that the velocities are in the inverse ratio to the masses; hence, if we have a gun 200 times heavier than the projectile, the recoil will not exceed the $\frac{1}{200}$ of that which it would have been in the purely theoretical hypothesis, where the gun was supposed to be of the same weight as the projectile.

"Very light guns have a great recoil, and quickly destroy their carriages. Very heavy guns have easy recoil, but are deprived of facility of manœuvering, a quality very essential to their use in service.

"It was thought that the recoil of a cannon must necessarily affect the velocity, and consequently the range of the ball; but all experiments tending to elucidate this point go to show that with cannon the recoil is not apparent in its effect upon the velocity of the ball. Hutton says, referring to some experiments on this subject, 'Varying the weight of the gun produced no change in the velocity of the ball.'"

THE HERCULES GUN.

Page 119—"On board of a ship, the limited space that we have at command in the rear of the battery, renders it necessary to restrain the recoil within certain limits. We see, therefore, that we must diminish the recoil, either by *friction properly managed*, or by the *elasticity of cordage*."

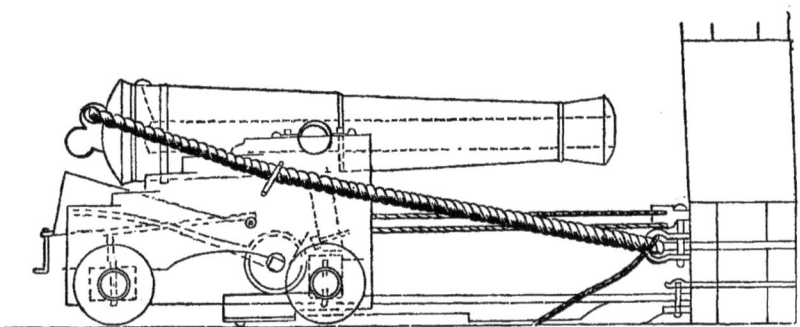

Present style of Naval Gun and method of preventing recoil.

On page 432, the General continues:

"If it shall be found that we can obtain good results with lighter guns, it will be desirable to adopt them, in order to free the ship of so much weight on deck, and the weight of the guns now not being sufficient to control the recoil, the field would seem to be thrown open for the invention of means to control the recoil."

Now, let us stick a pin right here!

The great PEACE-MAKERS give no trouble in this respect.

Almost all of the recoil here complained of is absorbed by the recoil cushion in the breech of the Dr. McLEAN arms, and the balance of the recoil is taken up by other devices connected with the gun!

If these wonderful guns possessed no other merit, this alone is a sufficient reason why every government must and will adopt them. But the absorption of the recoil is only *one* of the many improvements over the present style of guns which are concentrated in these WONDERFUL ARMS.

THE DEFECT OF "WINDAGE" INSEPARABLE FROM MUZZLE LOADERS.

In order to secure the best results for a shot, it should have as little windage as possible; that is, it should fit the barrel snugly, hence if a ball be as closely a fitting one as is requisite to reduce the windage to a minimum, then it is almost impossible to ram it securely home from the muzzle, for if a shot be not securely seated upon the powder, a bursting of the gun is almost sure to follow its discharge.

Of the evils of windage Gen. SIMPSON says:

Page 84—"*Windage*" impairs the accuracy of fire, and occasions a great loss of gas, which diminishes the effect of the charge; it is also the principal cause of the deterioration of cannon."

WINDAGE WASTES ONE-THIRD OF THE POWDER ENERGY.

Page 185—"Experiments made with the ballistic pendulums show that four pounds of powder, *without windage*, was found to give a ball nearly as great a velocity as six pounds of powder with a windage of $\frac{14}{100}$ths of an inch. Thus windage causes the loss of nearly *one-third the force of the charge.*"

Pages 188 to 191—"The strain on a gun is due to the resistance that is offered by the projectile to the expansion of the gases on the ignition of the charge; the greater this resistance, the greater will be the effect, to burst the gun. In other words, the more rapidly the projectile takes up its progressive motion, the less will be the strain exerted upon the gun. Now, if the diameter of the ball be such as to fill up the entire diameter of the bore, the gases will direct their whole force to propel the ball toward the muzzle; and in this way the pressure upon the gun will be the soonest relieved, and the strain will be the least possible.

"If, however, the ball *does not* fill up the entire diameter of the bore, but an opening is left between the upper hemisphere of the ball and the bore, the gases will not exert all their force to propel the ball toward the muzzle, but a portion of them will find vent through the windage ring, thus *exerting a force on the top side of the ball*, pressing it down on the lower side of the bore, and increasing its resistance to the propelling force by the friction generated through the means of this pressure.

"The resistance to the expansion of the gases is thus increased, and the consequence must be an increased strain upon the gun.

"A musket was loaded with a loose ball and a large charge of powder. On firing the charge, the ball, instead of proceeding out through the muzzle,

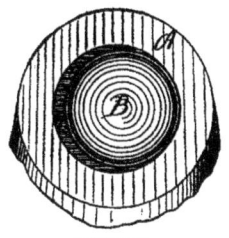

WINDAGE.
A. End view of Cannon.
B. Ball showing Windage.

tore a passage for itself through the *under part of the barrel*, coming out just below the middle band. The gas, rushing between the ball and the upper part of the bore, exerted such a retarding and downward pressure as to produce the above extraordinary result."

BY THESE UNIMPEACHABLE WITNESSES MUZZLE-LOADERS STAND FOREVER CONDEMNED!

All of the terrible accidents that have occurred through the bursting of cannon happened to muzzle-loaders, and it is probable that nine-tenths of such burstings were caused by windage.

Read over again the above statement of the loose musket ball bursting through the side of the barrel! Do reasoning minds hesitate to condemn unqualifiedly all muzzle-loading arms after reading such conclusive testimony as the above?

What is proven by the above extracts?

It is proven that windage is criminally wasteful, for $33\frac{1}{3}$ per cent. more powder is required to produce a result with windage, than is needed to produce the same result *without windage!*

It is proven that windage is criminally destructive of life and property by causing the bursting of guns.

In the face of this fact, what statesman or what manner of soldier dare advocate the longer continuance of muzzle-loading guns in any service.

Away with them!

They are wasteful, treacherous and destructive.

Convert them all into the Dr. J. H. McLEAN LIGHTNING BREECH-LOADERS.

With these admirable arms no windage is possible.

DEFECT IN THE POSITION OF THE TRUNNIONS.

The trunnions are the two short arms cast upon the sides of guns as they are now constructed, and it is intended to prove, by the best military writers, that they are a source of great weakness in guns.

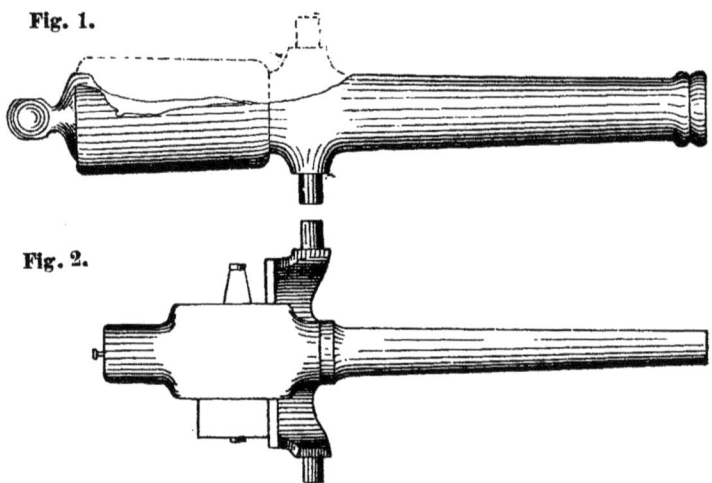

Fig. 1. BURSTED GUN. The trouble began at the vent, and the line of severance reveals the weak parts.

Fig. 2. Dr. J. H. McLEAN'S HERCULES GUN.

On page 113, Gen. SIMPSON says:

"Another great cause of the want of strength in guns, as at present formed, is the position of the trunnions, as regards the point to which the recoil of the gun is transmitted. The existence of these trunnions, by forming great re-entering angles on the surface of the gun, is of itself a great cause of weakness, for the following reason: The force exerted to produce recoil, acting as a pressure against the interior of the breech, is propagated as a force tending to stretch the metal of the gun along its whole length toward the muzzle; the rate of propagation being extremely rapid, so much so that to the senses the whole gun recoils together, and as one mass, and at the same instant; *yet in reality the first effect of the recoil is to elongate the gun, pushing out the breech part like one end of a spiral spring.* * * *

"If the gun be fixed rigidly on trunnions *placed in the usual position*, the strain tending to tear or break them off is equal to the whole work done by the recoil."

Right here, again, Dr. J. H. McLEAN may be permitted to shout out EUREKA!

The barrels of his Peace-makers have no trunnions upon them!

The breech parts of his guns have no trunnions upon them, but the trunnions are cast upon a bed plate connected with the breech, but so arranged that the trunnions are no longer an element of weakness.

Look on the foregoing picture and judge for yourself.

This feature alone would recommend Dr. McLean's Peace-makers to every nation on the earth, yet it is comparatively an unimportant one in these magnificent guns.

THE DEFECT OF AN INELASTIC CHAMBER.

The chamber of a gun is that portion in which the charge is exploded, and one of the most serious obstacles in the way of enlarging the weight of a projectile is that its *inertia* is so vastly increased by increasing its diameter, that before this inertia can be overcome by the pressure which the inflamed powder exerts upon it, the formation of gas by the burning powder is so rapid, and the development of force by the confinement of the gas is so great, that the strain upon the gun becomes fearful.

A pound of powder burned in the open air develops but little force, because the air is easily shoved aside to make room for the volume of gas so instantaneously formed.

A pound of powder burned in the tube of a gun develops more force, because the gas is confined by the metal, and can only get room to expand by driving the air in its front out of the tube.

A pound of powder burned in a metal tube behind a wooden plug develops still more force, because the plug will not move out of the way as quickly as the air would, alone, and thus give the gas room to expand.

A pound of powder burned in a metal tube behind a heavy metal projectile, develops still more force, because the metal cannot be made to move forward as promptly as the wooden plug can. Continue to increase the weight of this metal, and it soon becomes a question as to which will give way the quickest, the metal tube or the projectile.

It will be seen, then, that the defect of an *inelastic chamber* is a very grave defect, and it is one which has hitherto been supposed wholly irremediable.

Listen to what the military writers have to say about it. On page 186 Gen. SIMPSON says:

"In 1833 Capt. Piobert invented an *elastic wad*, to be placed between the ball and the powder where large charges were used, so as to *give increased space* for the formation of the gas, and save the guns from bursting."

GIBBONS MANUAL, page 96, says:

"The yielding of the ball, when a piece is fired, gives the inflamed gases an opportunity to expand, and prevents their energy being expended upon the piece.

"* * * * *If a gun could be* made of elastic material, which yielding to the first force of the powder without breaking, would give time for a sufficient force to be developed to expel the ball, injurious effects upon the piece would not result."

So deeply impressed with the defects of an inelastic chamber was the author of "Gibbon's Manual," that he devotes several pages of his work explaining the evil—an evil which he supposed never could be overcome. On pages 92 to 94 the following is found:

"In artillery practice, the restraining power which causes the powder to act against the walls of the cannon, is derived principally from the inertia of the shot. Now, let us compare the difference of the force of powder as exerted upon a small and a large gun respectively. It is perfectly well known that if we have a pipe or hollow cylinder of, say, two inches in diameter, with walls an inch thick, and if this cylinder will bear a pressure from within of 1,000 pounds per inch, another cylinder of the same material of ten inches in diameter will bear the same number of pounds to the inch if we increase the walls in the same proportion, or make them five inches thick. A cross section of these cylinders will present an area proportional to the squares of their diameters, and if the pressure be produced by the weight of plungers or pistons, as in the hydrostatic press, the weight required in the pistons will be as the squares of the diameters, or as four to one hundred.

"Now, carry this to two cannon of different calibers, and take an extreme case. Suppose the caliber of one to be two inches in diameter, and the other ten inches, and that the sides of each gun equal in thickness, the diameter of its caliber. Then, to develop the same force per inch, from the powder of each gun, the inertia of the balls should be as the squares of the diameters of the calibers, respectively; that is, one should be twenty-five times as great as the other. But one of the balls being two inches and the other ten inches in diameter, will weigh 1 pound and 125 pounds respectively; the weights being as the cubes of the diameters, 8 to 1,000, or 1 to 125. Hence each inch of powder in the large gun will be opposed by five times as much inertia as is found in the small gun.

"This produces a state of things precisely similar to that of loading the small gun with five balls instead of one; and although the strain thrown upon the gun by five balls is by no means five times as great as that by one ball, there can be no doubt that the strain produced by different weights of ball is in a ratio as high as that of the cube roots of the respective weights. This would give, in the example before us, of from 1 to 1.71, or the stress upon the walls of the ten inch gun would be seventy-one per cent. greater than upon those of the two inch gun.

* * * * * * * * *

"Whether the charge be large or small, the motion of the shot commences while the pressure is the same in both cases, and before the charge is fully burned, and with the same velocity in both cases; but with the large charge the fluid is formed faster than with the small, while the enlargement of the cavity by the movement of the shot is nearly the same in both cases."

THE ELASTIC CHAMBER OF THE PEACE-MAKERS!

Again Dr. J. H. McLean is entitled to run up his flag and fire a salute from a whole battery of Hercules guns in his own honor!

Why? Because he has solved the grand problem, and presents to the world a cannon with an elastic chamber?

You don't believe it! No; of course you don't believe it. All the more unfortunate for you; for it is a FACT, and in these days of lightning progress he who disputes facts is so irreclaimably an idiot as to miss even the contempt of the thinking and the candid.

Yes! wonderful as the announcement may seem, it is a fact that Dr. J. H. McLean presents to the world guns and small arms with a contrivance which enlarges the powder chamber at the instant of the discharge, enabling the gas to have increased room while overcoming the inertia of the projectile, thus reducing the recoil and the strain upon the gun!

There! match these guns who can!

This contrivance is the recoil cushion. Against this cushion the steel shell containing the charge is violently forced, and the cushion yields sooner than the projectile does. It is compressed, the chamber is greatly enlarged, and the gun is cocked!

THERE, AGAIN! MATCH THESE WONDERFUL GUNS WHO CAN!

DEFECTS OF THE OLD FASHIONED VENT.

Did you ever hear a gun hang fire?

P—i—s—h—h—h—h——bang!

There's the old fashioned vent for you. A battle-line might throw itself flat, clean out of harm's way, after the match is applied before the fire is actually communicated to the charge.

And the greater the gun the greater is the evil; for the distance *through the vent* to the charge is correspondingly increased, and so is the time which elapses while the priming is burning.

Gen. GIBBON, in his "Manual," pages 452, 453, says:

"In the practice of naval gunnery it is most particularly important that the actual delivery of the charge from the piece should follow as instantaneously as possible *the action of the lock*, for whilst the object aimed at is continually changing its relative position, the direction of the gun is varying so rapidly that if the medium that is to convey ignition to the charge act not very rapidly, the angle of the shot's departure may be two or three degrees above or below that at which the gun was pointed when the lock-string was pulled.

" * * * * It is therefore *vastly important* to use those means that are best calculated to produce the most instantaneous discharge possible."

Several methods of firing guns are employed, though all ways include the objectionable "*Vent.*" Field artillery is fired by a quill or brass primer. This is thrust into the vent, and being filled with a fulminate and a rough wire to produce friction, is a handy way, which is all that can be said of it. The percussion locks once so universally used on field pieces were discarded for the handier primer, but the attempt to use the primers in the navy was abandoned for reasons thus given by Gen. GIBBON on page 280 of his "Manual."

"The objection to adopting these primers on board ship is the damage that may be done by the flying of the brass tubes, which issue from the vent with great force when the piece is discharged. In action, the crew generally dispense with their shoes, and many might be sersously disabled by the sharp pieces of brass lying on the deck under their feet."

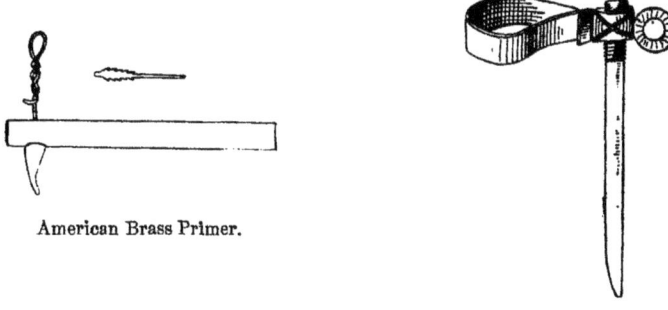

American Brass Primer.   English Quill Primer.

But a more serious charge is brought against the vent by Gen. GIBBON than the mere retarding the fire of the gun. On page 98, he says:

"During a heavily sustained fire the *vents* of guns enlarge. They take an irregular and angular form, and it is worthy of note that when a piece bursts, the plane of rupture nearly always passes through this orifice *and begins at it*. The crack from the vent has been found to increase gradually up to a certain time before the bursting takes place, and has been known to be arrested by the boring of a new vent."

So, then! the vents are not only laggards in firing, but they are *assassins as well;* taking the life of the poor old gun, eventually, and with it, almost always, the more precious lives of—GUNNERS!

A plague upon the old vents!

Away with them forever!

Dr. J. H. McLEAN's Peace-makers know them not!

Ah; no, indeed!

No slow old vents—no lurking assassins for the great Peace-makers!

The charges for the Peace-makers are enclosed in steel shells, and every shell is supplied with an unfailing primer of a new construction.

Shove in the shell! Press the trigger!

BANG!

The great gun is fired as quick as a lightning's flash!

A movement of the hand—out pops the shell into its receptacle and in goes another.

The gun is already cocked? Touch the trigger!

BANG!

The giant Hercules speaks again! A child may make it talk!

Ah, men and brethren, we say unto you once more, *match these wonderful guns who can!*

Gen. GIBBON says, on page 170:

"It would appear that the direction of the vent, in order to produce more rapid combustion, ought to terminate at the center of the bottom of the charge, or in the direction of the axis."

The Peace-makers are all "*central fire;*" therefore this other want of Gen. GIBBON is fully supplied.

Having fully pointed out and *proved up* the many defects in the cannon of the present make, it only remains, now, to more fully describe the

CONSTRUCTION OF THE WONDERFUL PEACE-MAKERS.

By reference to the engraving of the Hercules guns a trough will be noticed fixed, at a gentle upward incline, to the barrel of the gun. There are two of these troughs, one on each side. These troughs have numerous pulleys or little wheels in the bottom and along the sides, over which the heavy shot in the smooth steel shells rapidly and easily glide to the slide into which they are successively forced by the weight of the shot above them in the trough, as each in its turn becomes the bottom shot.

In the center of the rear face of the steel shell is a percussion primer, upon which a firing bolt, running through the breech of the gun, strikes and fires the charge. The recoil of the charge cocks the gun, runs it backward up the inclined ways shown in the engraving, and as it returns to position, ingenious machinery underneath it and connected with the slide moves a new charge in, ready for firing, and the empty shell out.

THE HERCULES GUN. 117

Dr. J. H. McLean's Hercules Guns Mounted in an Earthwork Throwing Projectile Torpedoes at a Fleet.

Thus this immense gun is converted not only into a breech-loader, but into a magazine gun which can be fired four times faster than any breech-loading cannon now in the world. Dr. J. H. McLean challenges the world to surpass these formidable guns.

OLD GUNS CAN BE CONVERTED INTO THE WONDERFUL PEACE-MAKERS.

And the best of it is *that all of the sound cannon, of whatever length or caliber, can easily* and cheaply be converted into these terrible death-dealing weapons. The amount saved to every nation by this fact will be enormous, as a single new gun of large size costs from $50,000 to $100,000. Krupp has just completed a big steel breech-loader at Meppen, weighing 72 tons. The cost of the raw material alone, at 18 cents per pound, would be $25,920. The labor put upon such a gun is worth many times the cost of the raw material; consequently, it is safe to conclude, this gun of Krupp's cost a good deal more than $100,000. It is said the shot of this gun will weigh 1,600 pounds, and with 380 pounds of powder can be thrown 11 miles, and a Hercules gun will throw its shot still further. By reference to the engraving showing Dr. McLean's Hercules guns, it will be seen that they are principally employed in throwing *projectile torpedoes*. These immense bolts are 13 to 17 feet in length, and will weigh 1,200 to 1,600 pounds and carry 100 pounds of electric powder, having all the power of nitro-glycerine and safe to handle. These torpedoes can be thrown many miles at vessels with a charge of 250 pounds of prismatic powder, and Dr. J. H. McLean is ready to give

A GOOD AND SUFFICIENT BOND OF $100,000 OR MORE,

that these torpedoes will utterly destroy in a few minutes any fleet of iron clads, no matter how secure they are armored, within range.

Any nation that will build a gunboat armed with one or more Hercules guns, 15 inches diameter, according to Dr. J. H. McLean's directions, for the throwing of these projectile torpedoes, will be guaranteed their successful working in a good and sufficient bond. The principle upon which these torpedoes are built is entirely new, and the reader will find a full description of them under their appropriate heading.

The big gun which Herr Krupp has just built, throws a shell weighing 1,600 lbs. and charged with 25 pounds of powder. This shell is not always sure to explode in the exact spot desired, nor just at the precise time desired, but Dr. J. H. McLean's time shells are guaranteed to explode at the precise spot and time wished. They can be timed to explode at from one second to three days, consequently none of them need be wasted. All such large shells are costly, and *every one* should be made to tell. In that memorable action which resulted in the

SINKING OF THE CONFEDERATE PRIVATEER ALABAMA

by the U. S. war vessel Kearsarge, the Alabama sent a hundred pound shell into the stern of the Kearsarge below the water line. It broke through the rudder post and lodged there, but did not explode. Had that shell been one of Dr. J. H. McLean's time shells, nothing could have saved the Kearsarge, for these shells are all charged with two or three small firing mechanisms each of (enveloped in thick rubber cases) which may be set to fire in one instant or in one week, from time of striking the object at which they are thrown. A full description of these powerful "peace-makers," and the reasons why they will be found to excel every other kind of shell now in use, will be found in the chapter devoted to projectiles.

THE LONG RANGE MANIA!

The Armstrong gun, it is claimed, can, under favorable conditions, throw a shot 9 miles or 14,840 yards, and 10,000 yards quite easily. This seems to have put Herr Krupp upon his metal, so to speak, and evidently he and his

German friends and backers determined not to be outdone, for it is claimed that his new steel gun, at an angle of 45 degrees, could throw its 1,600 pound projectile 15 miles or 25,400 yards! It is said the Meppen shooting ground has a range of only 11 miles, consequently it would never do for HERR KRUPP and his friends to work their gun up to its best pace. We must do HERR KRUPP and his friends the justice to state that they acknowledge that no object much smaller than a first class PLANET could be struck, except by accident, at such a distance, and that even at the forthcoming trial of the gun some means must be relied upon other than the visibility of the target, or very few "bull's eyes" will be scored.

This mania for "long range guns" is producing many wild statements. Six thousand yards, or a little less than 4 miles, is an excellent range for the largest guns, and when the "Swamp Angel," during the bombardment of Charleston, S. C., in the late civil war, pitched its shells 5 miles or 8,800 yards, the wonderful length of the range was a matter of comment all over the world.

When the large Armstrong guns were made, and a range of 10,000 yards actually proved for them, it was thought the limit was reached, and the military world are not and have not been ready to believe the subsequent statement that a range of 9 miles or 14,840 yards could be attained. Yet this seems but a stride compared with the 25,400 yards possibility of the new Krupp gun.

Dr. J. H. McLEAN's HERCULES GUNS will throw their projectiles just as far as any other gun of similar caliber and weight, and, owing to their elastic chambers, they can safely burn more powder than any other gun, therefore they will have a much longer range than any other, and they may be made of steel, or, what is still better, phosphor bronze, and guaranteed to to be more accurate than any other gun, and to be fired four times faster than any other guns of their size now manufactured. Whenever firing is too rapid to be accurate and effective it is simply a censurable waste of ammunition, therefore the Hercules guns are so constructed as to be completely under the control of "*one*" gunner. He is stationed upon a platform that moves backward with the gun when the recoil occurs. As the gun moves down the inclined plane to its position, the slide with its fresh charge by its own motive power is shoved into place, and the gun is ready to fire. No ramming, no swabbing, and no cocking is required. All the gunner has to do is to aim the piece and pull the trigger. To aid the accuracy of the aim, a long tube furnished with telescope lenses is fixed upon the breech of the gun in a position to be easily glanced through by the gunner. A little practice will enable him to keep his gun constantly bearing upon the mark, and to discharge his ponderous and terrible weapon with telling effect several times in a minute. The steel shells used to contain the powder and projectiles of these guns, may be "chambered," and in addition to this "chambering" the patented recoil mechanism in the breech gives the powder more room and more air, and consequently a perfect combustion is attained, and better results in every way are secured than are possible with guns now in use.

THE PEACE-MAKERS CANNOT BE BURSTED.

It is also claimed that Dr. J. H. McLean's Hercules guns, and his fire-arms of all descriptions and sizes, can burn heavier charges of powder and throw heavier projectiles, in comparison to their weight and caliber, without danger of bursting, than any guns now in use. The reasons for this assumption are four, as follows:

1.—The powder is put into a steel shell.

2.—The steel shell is put into a steel slide.

3.—The steel slide is shoved into a steel breech.

4.—A large part of the blow given to other guns when the charge is fired is taken up by the recoil mechanism provided for Dr. J. H. McLean's guns.

Supplementary reasons exist, and may be stated as follows:

The explosion and combustion of the powder takes place inside of a steel shell, and this shell is inside of a steel slide, consequently this slide does not get heated by the firing, no matter how long continued nor how rapid it may be, as a fresh and cold shell is inserted in the slide every time the gun is discharged.

HOW HEATING BREAKS METAL.

The expansion and shrinkage of metal soon causes it to weaken and crack. Take a piece of wire between the thumbs and fingers of each hand, and bend it back and forth rapidly in one spot a few times. It grows hot in that spot, cracks and finally breaks. So it is with a cannon. If that portion of the breech where the charge explodes is permitted to get very hot, as it is sure to do if fired rapidly, it is weakened every time this occurs, and it grows brittle, and sooner or later will burst and kill more or less of the persons using it. But the Dr. J. H. McLean arms never heat in the breech. The barrel is made separately from the breech and is screwed into it and may get hot—undoubtedly would—but it could not communicate any very great degree of heat to the slide, and none whatever to the shell in which the charge safely reposes. The barrel will not burst unless the breech does, but even if it did, not very much damage could be done, as the fragments would fly forward to the right and left of the gun, and not backward. As the gun is a breech-loader, there would be no men stationed to the right and left of the barrel, as is the case with muzzle-loaders.

HOW THE SHELL AND SLIDE PREVENT BURSTING.

It may be asked why the shell and the slide diminish the liability of bursting. Because, when the shell is in the slide and the slide, is in the gun, there are three distinct surfaces to be fractured: the shell, the slide, and the breech. If the reader will take three plates of cast iron half an inch thick, with perfectly smooth surfaces, and lay one upon the other, he will find it will take a much more severe blow to shatter all three than it would to shatter one solid plate of similar iron three times as thick. A rupture of the cohesion of the molecules (in the metal) is caused by vibration, and when there is a break in the continuity of the molecules vibration is impaired. The regulated tramp of a company of men across a long bridge will cause a vibration so powerful as to wreck the structure, however strong it may be, hence regulated marching is forbidden while crossing bridges. The same law holds good in the Dr. J. H. McLean arms. The first shock of the blow struck by the powder comes upon the shell; it is imperfectly transmitted to the slide, and still more imperfectly transmitted to the breech itself.

We have said the first shock falls upon the shell, but the shell darts backward out of the slide into the breech, against the recoil cushion, and back again into the slide, so that a large part of the blow is taken up by the recoil cushion, thus, altogether, making these guns the safest and most effective arms ever offered to the world.

To be put to the proof on all these points Dr. J. H. McLean challenges every Government in the World.

MAGAZINE CANNON.

QUITE recently General HANCOCK declared it to be his opinion that magazine arms were rapidly becoming indispensable in war, and those nations that provided themselves with the most effective weapons of this class would be strongest in battle. The application of magazines to shoulder guns has been making progress many years. All of the leading manufacturing nations have produced magazine arms of more or less value, but it has remained for Dr. J. H. McLEAN to give to the world the first magazine cannon ever known, and to bring to their highest perfection magazine arms of every description. While rapidity of fire is an essential point in improved arms of all descriptions, the mere ability to grind out cartridges by the bushel, without reference to effectiveness, is a poor recommendation for any weapon.

Before passing to a detailed description of the peculiar excellencies of these remarkable guns, it may be well to introduce the opinions of military writers upon field pieces and their uses.

IMPORTANCE OF ACCURACY OF FIRE.

Gen. GIBBON, on page 342 of his Manual, says:

"It is of the first importance that the fire of a battery be delivered at a good range, with calmness and intelligence. There are some circumstances, however, where several pieces well harnessed may advance to within 300 yards of an enemy and overwhelm him with a storm of grape or canister shot; but these cases are very rare and require much tact and resolution to know how to profit by them.

"One of the most brilliant feats of this kind probably ever performed on a field of battle occurred at the battle of Palo Alto, with Col. DUNCAN, who, by a well timed movement of two pieces of his battery, unlimbered in front of a large force of Mexicans attempting to turn the left flank of our line, and by a rapid and well sustained fire, drove them back in confusion."

Consider well what is stated above: "It is of the *first* importance" says Gen. Gibbon, "that the fire of a battery be delivered at a good range, with calmness and intelligence."

Agreed!

Now let the reader be informed what, in the General's estimation, constitutes a *good range*. On page 231 he remarks:

"Beyond the limit of distinct vision all fires become inexact. Field pieces should not fire at infantry beyond 1,000 yards, nor at cavalry beyond 1,200 yards."

This is exactly the position taken by Dr. McLean, namely, that this straining after long ranges is all nonsense, except where a city or fortified position of large area is to be shelled.

Agreed, then, as to the range.

At 1,000 or 1,200 yards the Dr. McLean magazine field pieces are the most deadly weapons in the shape of artillery that were ever trained upon a line of battle.

The fact of their never being thrown out of line by the recoil, as other guns are, enables the gunner to keep the range without any difficulty, and the fact that no swabbing or loading is necessary, enables the gunner to deliver his fire with that "calmness and intelligence" deemed so indispensable by Gen. Gibbon.

Read over again what the Gen. says respecting Col. Duncan's daring achievement at Palo Alto.

It is clear that while this *successful* dash commands the admiration of the General, such hazardous ventures are not advised.

But it has been one of the aims of Dr. McLean to provide field guns exactly fitted for such *artillery charges*.

Examine the manner in which the "Gen. Grant" and the "McLean Annihilator" are mounted.

NO LIMBERING OR UNLIMBERING REQUIRED THERE!

No exposing of half a dozen nervous and excited swabbers and loaders to the point blank fire of a battle line of rifles! See cut of such an action on next page.

126   Dr. J. H. McLEAN'S PEACE-MAKERS.

A Battery of the Cannon of To-Day in Action.—Look at the Number of Men Exposed.

There are ample charges in the magazines. The gun needs no swabbing.

Not even the gunner is fully exposed.

He stands upon the step of his carriage beyond the steel foundations of his admirable gun, and, ordering his piece up to within 200 yards of a battle line, "calmly and intelligently" pours in the most terrific broadsides ever sent from the throat of a gun. From forty-eight cannon balls a minute up to fifteen hundred and eighty-four every minute, how many seconds will a battle line stand such a fire delivered from a score or more such guns? See cut of a supposed action with these guns on the following page.

On another portion of page 342, the General from whom we are quoting says:

"Within 600 yards the firing *should be rapid, as it is then very sure.* * *

"Generally the rate of firing should be much less than one shot per minute.

"Volleys should not be fired, especially with small batteries,* *as the enemy is enabled to take advantage of the intervals between them to charge.*"

THE ANNIHILATING POWER OF THE PEACE-MAKERS!

If the firing of the old-fashioned artillery is sure, at 600 yards, as Gen. GIBBON says it is, by what adjective can the fire from the MCLEAN MAGAZINE GUNS be characterized at 200 yards?

It would be mild to say terrible! awful! aye, even devilish!

When it is considered that an ordinary field piece of present construction and mounting will run backward on its wheels at least ten feet when fired, and that it must be loaded at the muzzle, and swabbed and oiled before loading, brought back into position and sighted before firing, it is not to be wondered that "much less than one shot per minute" is recommended by Gen. GIBBON.

All of that nonsense is done away with by the "MCLEAN MAGAZINE FIELD PIECES."

---

* A battery consists of two to eight pieces, and a small battery is one of less than six pieces.

A Battery of Dr. J. H. McLean's Magazine Cannon in Action.—Only One Man to Each Gun Partially Exposed.

There have been battles where many thousand men, mounted upon as many thousand horses, charged the lines in a battle; but with comparatively little effect.

Let us suppose that one thousand of the McLean Magazine Field Pieces, accompanied by 5,000 men and 10,000 horses, were ordered to charge up to within 200 yards of a battle line, and each gun to pour in grape, canister and shell as rapidly as possible for ten minutes?

What sort of a tale would there be to tell about that battle?

Horrible! Horrible!! Horrible!!!

Gen. Gibbon says the firing of artillery should not be by volleys, lest the enemy take advantage of the interval required to load, rush upon the guns and capture them.

The McLean Magazine Field Pieces may be fired by volleys, and woe be to any troops that attempt to charge them.

ARTILLERY CANNOT DEFEND ITSELF.

On page 335 of his Manual, Gen. Gibbon, says:

"Artillery cannot defend itself when hard pressed, and should always be sustained by either infantry or cavalry. The proposition to arm the cannoneers with small arms, such as revolvers, short rifles, &c., is calculated to do more harm than good. They should be taught to look upon their pieces as their proper arm of defense, to be abandoned only at the very last moment. *The fate of many a battle has turned upon the delivery of a few rapid rounds of grape or canister at short range upon an advancing column.*"

It is true enough that artillery as at present constructed *cannot defend itself*, and that is the precise reason why Dr. McLean has such good grounds for congratulating the World upon the invention of his magazine field pieces.

THEY CAN DEFEND THEMSELVES!

And not only can they defend themselves, but they can turn the fate of many a battle "by the delivery of rapid rounds of grape and canister at short range."

Doubtless the reader is amply convinced of the insufficiency of the artillery in present use, and we may now venture upon a detailed

DESCRIPTION OF THE Dr. J. H. McLEAN'S MAGAZINE CANNON.

Dr. J. H. McLean's Magazine Cannon will be found to possess all of the desirable features, namely, accuracy, long range, rapid delivery, portability, and *to be so mounted that they can be effectively served while the horses are on a full run from one part of the field to another, or while being rapidly drawn by soldiers across a field parallel to the enemies' line of battle.*

This is flying artillery indeed! (See next page.)

In pursuit of an enemy these guns can be used with terrible effect while in rapid motion; no halt being required for the purpose of firing!

In retreat these guns are the salvation of an army and the terror of the enemy's dragoons!

Our first illustration of magazine cannon is called "THE GENERAL GRANT."

This is a two-inch rifled cannon, with a phosphor-bronze breech and a hammered Bessemer steel barrel. It has four magazines, and carries twelve shots in each, making 48 shots in all. These 48 shots can all be thrown from the gun in less than *one minute*, if necessary. For if a charge upon a battery of such guns is ever undertaken, the rapid delivery of 15 or 20 rounds from each gun at point blank range will either turn back or destroy any cavalry, dragoons or infantry, that would dare to make such a charge. Still the fact that 48 shots *can be thrown in less than a minute from this gun* adds immensely to its value as a peace-maker.

MAGAZINES IN RESERVE.

While being leisurely served in action it can be fired a good many times in a minute without drawing upon the reserves in the magazines at all, and if the situation is desperate, the 48 charges in the magazines can be used with highest rapidity, and four loaded magazines be substituted for the empty ones in a second of time, so to speak,

MAGAZINE CANNON.

Dr. J. H. McLean's Magazine Cannon galloping along a Line of Battle, Firing as it Goes.

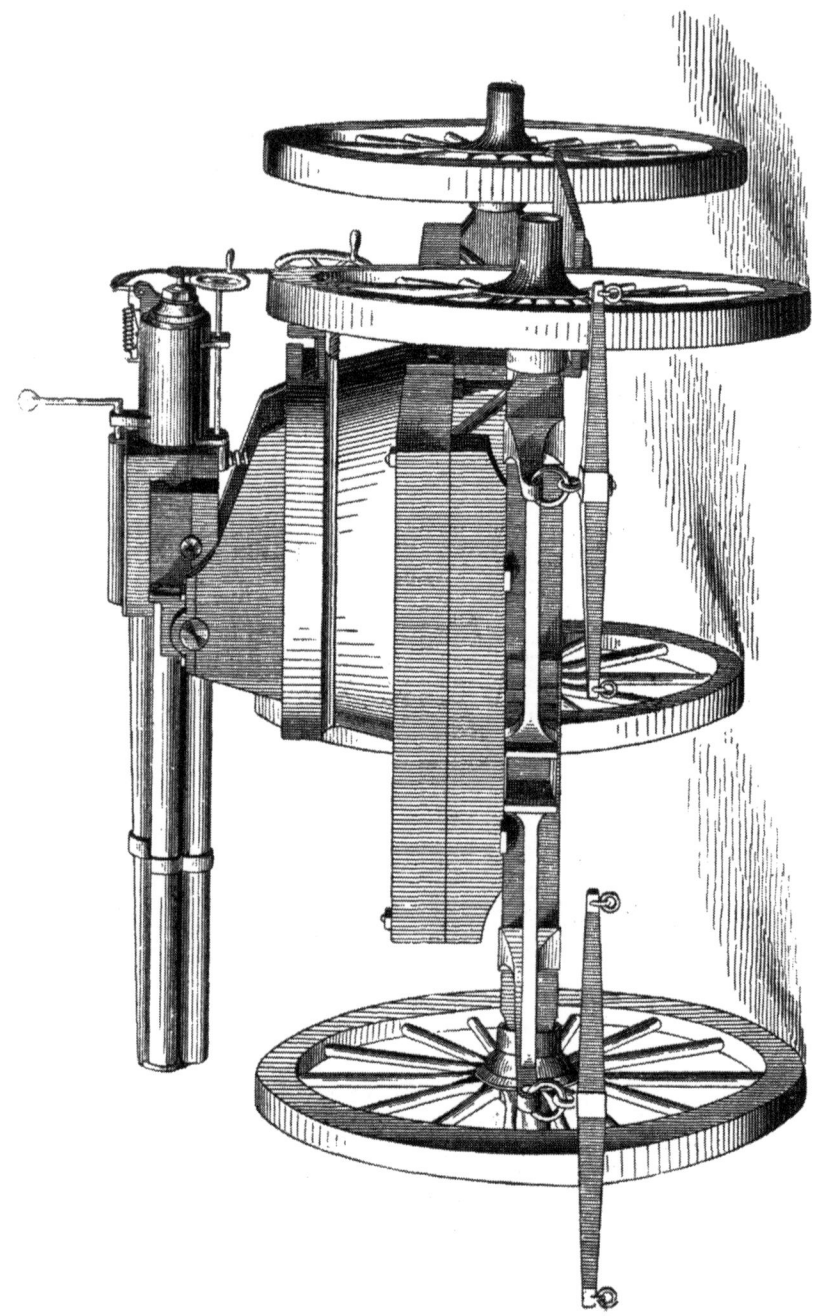

Dr. J. H. McLean's Magazine Cannon "General Grant."

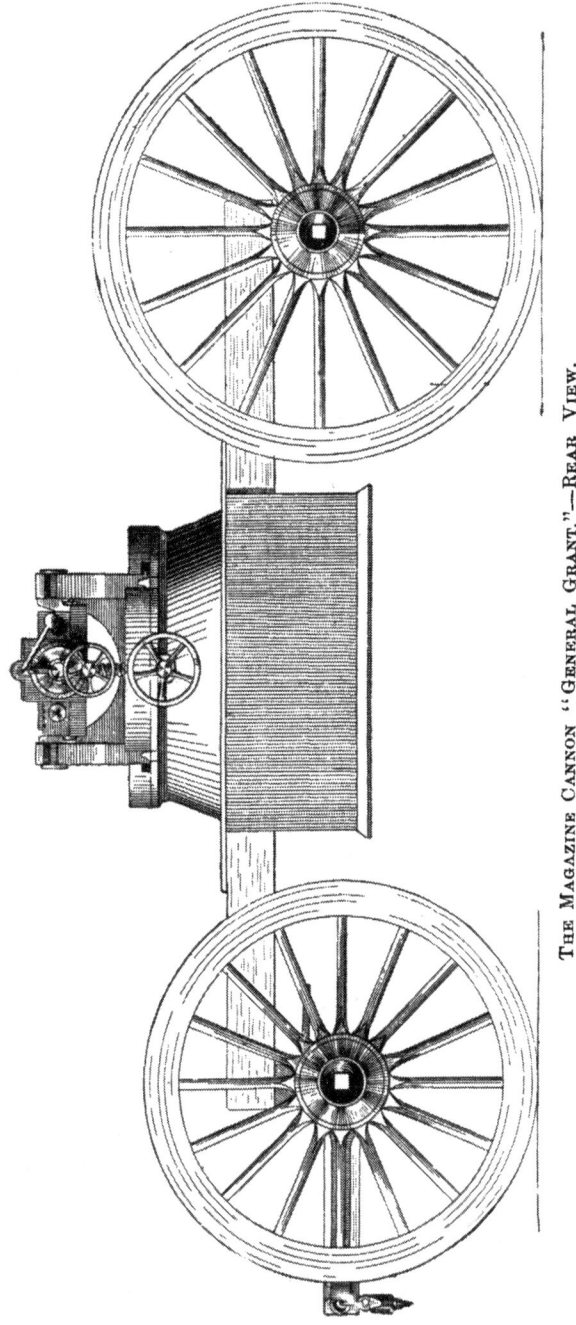

The Magazine Cannon "General Grant."—Rear View.

The caisson which accompanies these guns is so constructed as to carry several sets of magazines fully charged, and it is the work of but an instant to snatch the empty magazines out of their rests and replace them by filled ones. This can be done in much less time than is required to put a single charge in any of the breech-loading cannon as now constructed.

DISABLING THE GUN WHEN NECESSARY.

Another very important feature of Dr. J. H. McLEAN's Magazine and Breech-loading Cannon is, that they may be thoroughly disabled by *one man*, and rendered unfit for subsequent service.

One man can snatch out the slide and run away with it, and it is then entirely useless to the enemy. If in a hot contest all of the horses belonging to the gun are killed, and its capture becomes certain, one man, with a single turn of a handle, can release and remove the slide, and either conceal it or carry it off, and the captured gun becomes a poor trophy. The slide and guns are similarly numbered, so that when recaptured the guns are easily made serviceable again.

Contrast this easy and quick method with any one of the following ways of disabling a gun recommended in GIBBON's MANUAL.

Page 77. To render guns unserviceable:

"1st. Drive into the vent a jagged and hardened steel spike with a soft point, or a nail without a head; break it off flush with the outer surface and clinch the point inside by means of the rammer.

"2d. Wedge a shot in the bottom of the bore by wrapping it with felt, or by means of iron wedges; using the rammer or an iron bar to drive them in.

"3d. Cause shells to be burst in the bore of brass guns; or fire broken shot from them with high charges.

"4th. Fill a piece with sand over the charge and thus burst it.

"5th. Fire one piece against another, muzzle to muzzle, or the muzzle of one to the chase of the other.

"6th. Light a fire under the chase of a brass gun and strike on it with a sledge to bend it.

"7th. Break off the trunnions of iron guns, or burst them by firing them with heavy charges and full of shot at a high elevation."

THE ANNIHILATOR.

The Dr. J. H. McLean Annihilator, as shown in the accompanying engraving, is, beyond all doubt, the most extraordinary piece of ordnance ever invented. It is supplied with twelve magazines carrying ten charges each, and is therefore competent to deliver 120 rounds in rapid succession. As the cocking and firing are both made automatic, the piece may be discharged every second, or 60 times in one minute, if ever deemed necessary.

This remarkable gun is made of cast steel, and the one now on exhibition has a bore two inches in diameter. The barrel has a rifled bore, is 70 inches long, and screws into the breech. The magazines are cylindrical, and extend all around the gun. They can be all charged while on the gun quite as easily as off, and when in moderate use the charges in the magazines can be held in reserve for emergencies. The caissons are intended to carry several sets of fully charged magazines to be used in great emergencies, and the empty ones can be slipped off the gun, and loaded ones substituted, in much less time than is required to put one charge into a muzzle-loading cannon.

The "Annihilator" is intended, in this exhibition of Dr. J. H. McLean's Peace-Makers, to throw grape shot principally, and as no great accuracy or range is required, any sort of barrel may be used, but this being a steel rifled barrel is competent to throw shot, shell and grape, changing from one to the other at the will of the gunner! Brass, cast steel or cast iron barrels, any old guns, cast aside and worthless for any other purpose, can all be used in the manufacture of *Annihilators*, and thus convert worthless old metal into the most terribly destructive weapons.

No nation can afford to ignore this fact. What is true of the smoothbore barrels, is doubly true of the rifled ones. All sound cannon can be easily converted into good magazine cannon, and a large saving of money thereby effected.

In every nation a company can be established to convert all of the worthless arms belonging to the government into the efficient and unapproachable

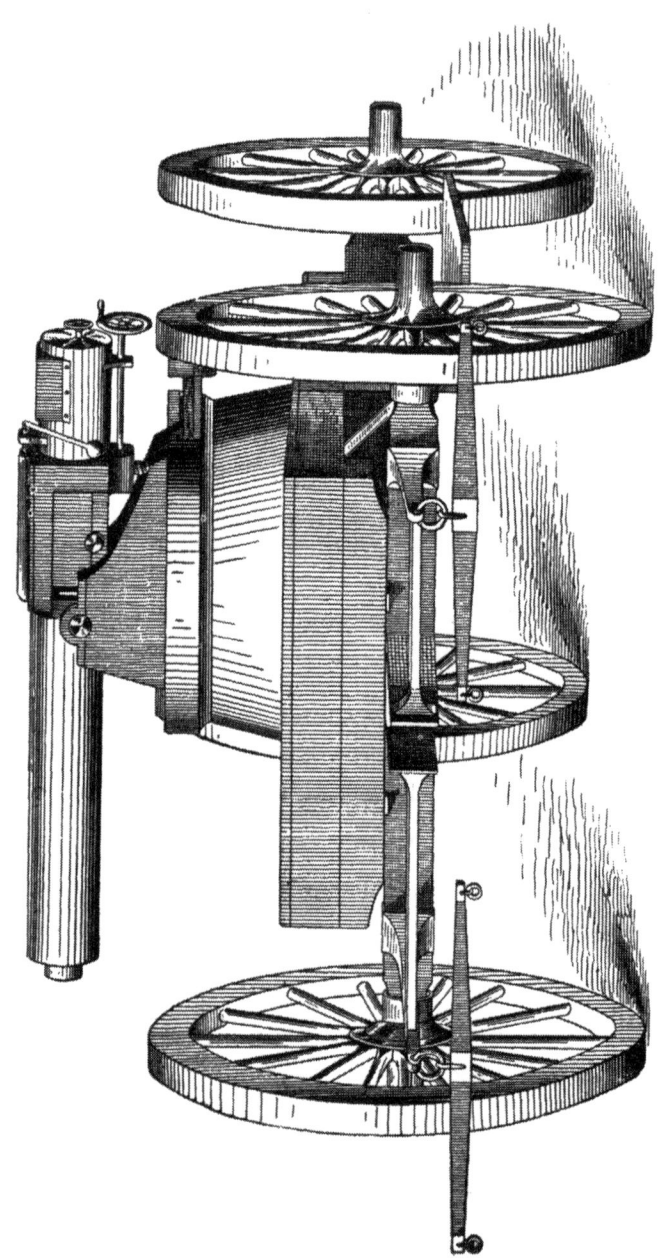

The Dr. J. H. McLean "Annihilator."—A Magazine Cannon Capable of Firing 120 Shots in a Minute!

MAGAZINE CANNON.

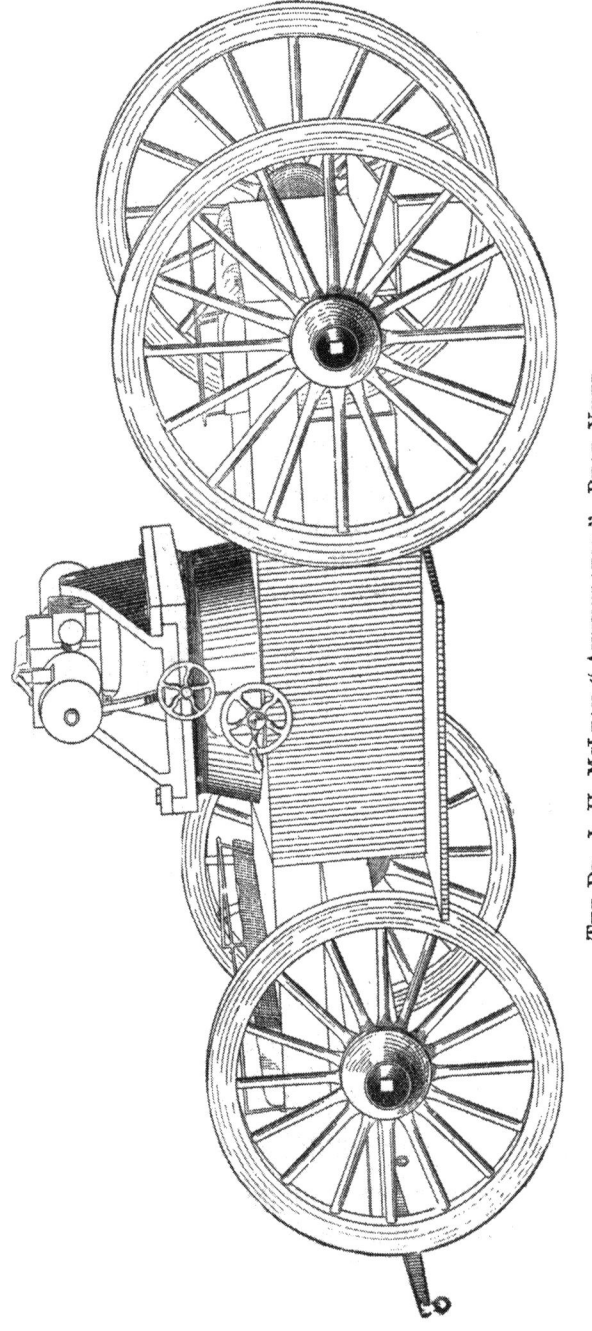

The Dr. J. H. McLean "Annihilator."—Rear View.

Dr. J. H. McLean's Peace-Makers; and while saving millions to the government, they will be making large fortunes for their stockholders.

THE AVAILABILITY OF OLD GUNS.

On pages 91 and 92, Gen. Gibbon has this to say respecting old guns:

"Three eight-inch columbiads, one of them newly cast and the other two cast six years previous and of inferior metal to the new one, were tried. The new one failed at the 72d round. The weakest of the old ones failed at the 800th round, while the other sustained 2582 rounds and was apparently as good as ever.

"Here is an apparent anomaly which appears to be satisfactorily explained by the supposition that the strain which has been referred to as assisting in the gun when cast is limited in duration, and that, like many other substances, iron possesses the property of accommodating itself to an unnatural position, and finally of adopting this as its natural one, and of actually being as strong or even stronger in that than in the original state; just as a wagon bow or barrel hoop, after becoming used to the new direction, will not only *not* return, when released, to the old, but require *force* to bring it back; showing that the fibres possess the power of accommodating themselves in accordance with the solicitation of external forces. There is nothing in the character of iron which precludes this idea of a new arrangement of the fibres; on the contrary, as has been shown, it does take place under certain circumstances."

There cannot be the least doubt but that every government possesses a greater or less number of old cannon of various calibers which can be converted at a reasonable expense into the McLean Magazine Artillery.

Smooth bores may be rifled, and all of the mistaken inequalities of surface upon the outside of the barrels can be easily turned off, and handsome and serviceable guns produced at very small cost.

In every nation companies formed for this purpose can make fortunes.

Cannon of the Annihilator pattern can be made 4 inches in diameter, to weigh not more than two tons. They may be mounted upon strong four wheeled wagons, as shown in the accompanying engraving, and successfully used in Indian warfare. Charged with grape shot they would have a deadly range of two miles, and can be fired with lightning-like rapidity, and served nearly as accurately when the carriage is in motion as when it is at rest. While the magazines are charged with grape cartridges, ball cartridges may be freely used by hand loading, if greater range than two miles is wanted, and, as the magazines are in pairs (6 pairs), solid shot may be put into two pairs, shells into two, and grape cartridges into two, and rounds from either pair fired at the will of the gunner.

Dr. J. H. McLean challenges the world to produce a weapon superior to this, and is ready at all times to meet contestants in public trial.

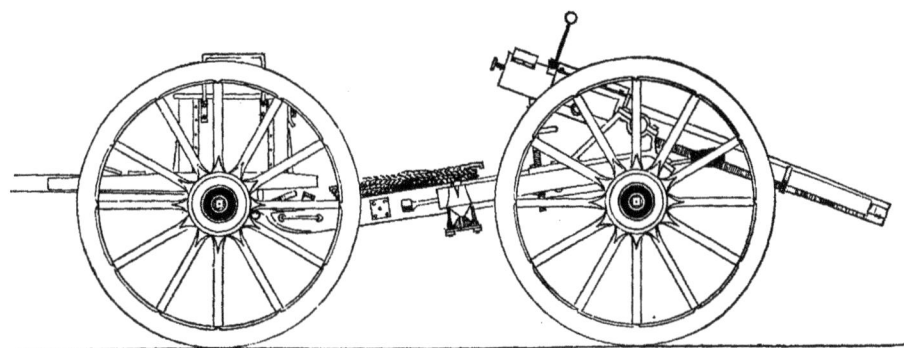

The Magazine Cannon "Vixen."

The accompanying engraving exhibits a light field piece, mounted in the old style, having a pair of magazines, only. Upon a four or six-inch gun of proper length these magazines will each carry 10 shots, giving twenty rounds for rapid delivery whenever emergency may demand; but, as is the case with the two preceding guns, these magazines need not be drawn upon the ordinary firing, and if emptied can quickly be replaced by filled ones from the caisson.

All of these magazine cannon are self-cocking, and are provided with the recoil breech-pins and automatic firing-slide, so that the gunner need only to give one push on the lever—

Bang! the gun is fired!

another push—

Bang! it is fired again!

and so on as rapidly as he may choose to work his lever.

WHY THE MAGAZINE CANNON WILL NOT WASTE AMMUNITION.

Nearly all military writers appear to labor under the apprehension that magazine arms of any description will only serve the useless purpose of enabling the gunner or soldier to consume more ammunition than is now consumed.

Artillery ammunition costs much money; therefore, while providing weapons that can be fired with lightning-like rapidity, Dr. J. H. McLean enters a protest against wild, excited and reckless shooting, and points out the fact that his Peace-Makers are eminently calculated to inculcate steadiness and coolness in action, and consequent good aim and excellent results.

Why? Because, first, but few men are exposed. The gunner is measurably protected, and having no nervous and excited "swabbers" in front of him to take up his attention and distract his aim, will be more certain to get his shot home and fire deliberately. Second, because the gunner has no excited "thumber of the vent" in his way. Third, because, as the gun-slide is always cool and always loaded, and the gunner realizes that he has but to make *one motion* to discharge his piece, he becomes filled with that steadiness which is always inspired by a sense of being master of the situation, and he will not foolishly and excitedly empty his magazines.

But with the common muzzle-loading cannon the "swabbers," "shot-passers," "thumbers," and all the squad at work about the gun are exposed, excited and nervous. They work with all the rapidity they can as a relief to their deadly fear, and the result is immense noise, great volumes of smoke, lots of costly ammunition wasted, and—that is all.

Occasionally a cannon shot *hits some one;* but it is safe to say, that for the ten to twenty thousand shot thrown, and fifty to one hundred thousand pounds of powder burned in a battle, not fifty men receive hurts in consequence.

But far different results are expected from the Dr. J. H. McLean's Peace-Makers. The secure feeling inspired by the certainty of *always being ready,* and of possessing the ability to deliver shots when the pinch comes with lightning-like rapidity, will surely develop great steadiness, coolness and good judgment in the men having such batteries in charge.

THE PEACE-MAKERS IN THE MOUNTAINS.

Dr. J. H. McLean's Magazine Cannon are especially adapted for warfare in countries that are mountainous, and rough and difficult to traverse with compact, old-fashioned artillery. The gun can be taken to pieces and packed upon horses, mules, elephants, camels, or asses. There are the breech, the slide, the breech pins, the barrel and the magazines, all separated, and in three minutes these parts can be put together and the gun be ready for action. For warfare in rough countries a mounting adapted for rude sledges has been devised. A rude, narrow sledge can be dragged up any mountain path where there is room for a horse or mule to walk, and with no weight on the sledge except the mountings of the gun, one horse or mule can pull it up the steepest roads. The ammunition for these guns consists of charged steel shells, and these can be packed in sacks or boxes and carried on the backs of pack animals quite easily and safely.

BATTERY GUNS.

By Battery Guns are meant those that have two or more barrels through which the loads are discharged simultaneously, or in rapid succession, and which are made light and portable, and convenient to use either in field-service or on shipboard. Some rude attempts to produce effective guns of this description have been made in different parts of the world, but it has thus far been demonstrated that the mechanism involved in the manufacture of such guns was too complicated and delicate to stand the rough usages of war.

EFFECTIVENESS OF BATTERY GUNS.

Everything finite has its limit. The limit to the size of a shoulder gun for army use is one of about 45 to 58 caliber, and the limit of its effective range is about 600 yards. Not that the gun may not be made to send its missile quite accurately double that distance, but at 600 yards a man on foot is quite as small a mark as the unaided eye is capable of striking, and to put a telescope sight on the rifle of each soldier would more than double the cost of the weapon and not increase the casualties in the enemy's ranks, because in action not one soldier in a hundred takes an aim at anything more definite than at the long line of smoke and dust which represents the enemy in his front.

How far away this line is he does not know. He loads his gun and fires as rapidly as he can until he is either ordered or driven from the field. What the effect of his firing has been he does not know. He is nervous and excited, and is constantly dreading the missile which is to kill or maim him.

With a line of battery guns quite a different condition of things exist. These guns throw balls of from three-quarters of an inch to an inch and a half in diameter, weighing from seven ounces to three pounds!

Each battery gun is furnished with a telescopic sight which enables the operator to distinctly view the men far beyond the battle line, where no smoke or dust hides them from view.

The telescope connected with a wind-guage and a spirit-level becomes a good RANGE FINDER, and gives the operator the approximate distance to the enemy.

HE IS MASTER OF THE SITUATION.

The operator is not nervous. He is in no way excited. He realizes that he is *master of the situation.*

He knows that he has but to make *one push of his lever to strew the whole earth in his front with dead.*

Hence he trembles not.

He is always ready.

He will deliver his fire not in frantic and wasteful haste, but with "*calmness, masterly skill and intelligence,*" *and awful havoc!*

He can smite the enemy *miles away!*

His dreadful weapon has all the accuracy of the rifle and the far-reaching sweep of the cannon!

ITS MISSILES ARE INVISIBLE AND CANNOT BE DODGED!

When the old style batteries are playing upon hostile lines the shot and shell are watched and *dodged;* but the swift and smaller missiles of the deadly Dr. McLEAN battery gun cannot be seen, and yet they reach as far and fly much truer than cannon-shot.

With every discharge of a 6-inch cannon 75 to 100 pounds of metal and 8 to 10 pounds of powder are wasted!

It is estimated that 10,000 rounds of rifle cartridges are used in killing or wounding *one man*, and the London (England) papers declare that a fair computation reveals the fact that it takes 5 active English riflemen 1½ hours steady firing to hit one Zulu!

If this is true in rifle shooting, what a wicked and enormous waste of powder and ball must be sustained by cannon firing in battle!

NOISE AS A TERRIFIER!

Army men admit that not one man is killed by cannon-shot in 20,000 rounds, but they advocate the continued use of cannon for the *moral effect* it has on the enemy!

" The noise frightens them ! "

The Chinese entertain the same belief, but they make their noise on gongs, which is, to say the least, *a good deal cheaper !*

Dr. J. H. McLean takes the ground that one of the main reasons why cannon are so ineffective is because of the excited condition of the gunners who are exposed to death in swabbing and loading, and in the mad desire to blaze away with great rapidity irrespective of results, in the belief that much noise and huge volumes of smoke are the true indications of valor in battle.

Read the preceding chapter on Magazine Cannon, and see if the Doctor is not right.

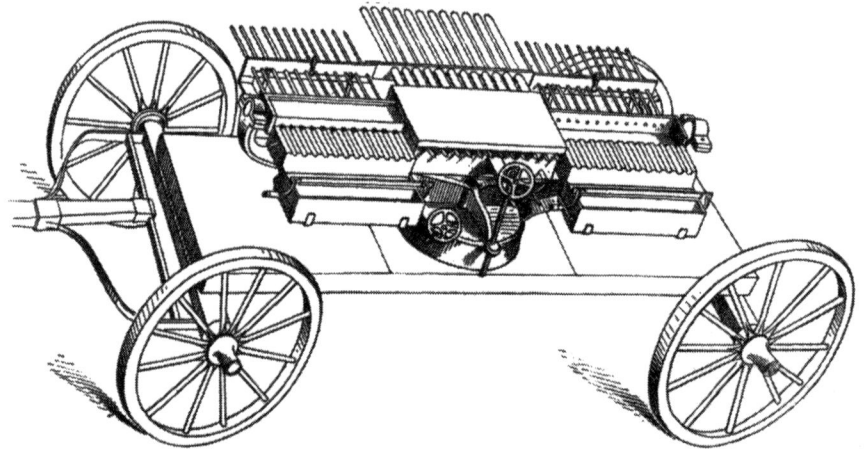

Dr. J. H. McLean's Hand-Loading Battery Gun "Besom."

THE BESOM.

Dr. J. H. McLean's battery guns are of two kinds: those with magazines and those without, and having 12 to 36 barrels to fire through. The engraving opposite shows a hand-loading battery.

This battery, the "Besom," has 12 barrels. It is a hand-loading battery, and is to be drawn by the men, and is mounted on a light-running gear, and should not exceed 50 to 70 caliber. This would insure a range of a mile or more, very effectively. Barrels to be rifled, and 32 to 38 inches long. It is a breech-loader, and may easily be discharged 30 times in a minute, thus throwing 360 shots with great force and precision. It is provided with recoil cushions, and is self-cocking. Steel shells are used, and they are swiftly put in and ejected. It can be rapidly served by five men, and is so simple in its construction that the dullest private can master everything about it in a minute. It will not get out of order, and only needs to be kept tolerably clean to do excellent work. This gun, made of cast steel, will not weigh more than 700 pounds, and can therefore be drawn by the men into very difficult positions, and served upon a battle-line with deadly effect. Horse-batteries of this make, with a caliber of 1 inch to $1\frac{1}{2}$ inches, with a range of three miles or more, would weigh about 3,000 pounds, and could be taken about by four horses, where any of the lightest artillery could be carried. The simplicity and serviceability of these guns, as well as their cheapness, will render them a general favorite. The Dr. J. H. McLean Arms Co. (wherever formed) can take the old rifle barrels of all calibers, and convert them into these truly formidable batteries at very little expense to a government entering into such a contract.

Let this important fact be borne in mind by the statesmen of all nations! All your old-fashioned arms can be made new.

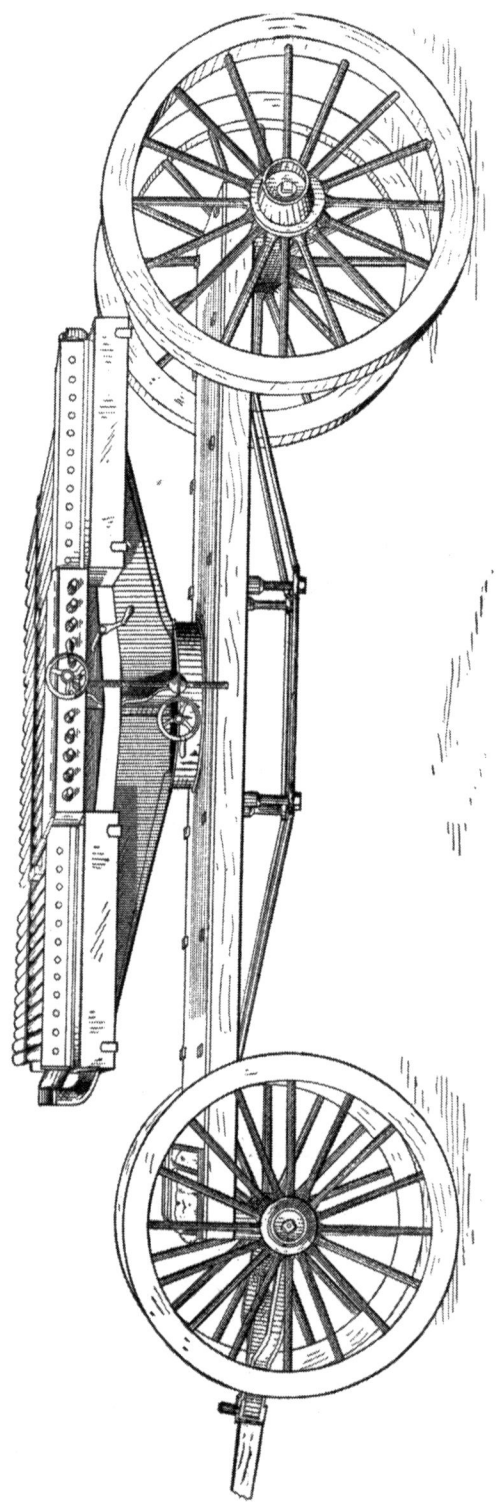

The Dr. J. H. McLean Magazine Battery Gun "Pulverizer," Capable of Throwing 1,200 Shots in a Minute!

BATTERY GUNS. 147

The "Pulverizer" in Action.

THE PULVERIZER.

The illustration on page 146, exhibit a battery gun similar to the one previously shown, except it is loaded by magazine tubes, and takes its charged shells in at the front side of the slide, and discharges the empty ones through the rear face of the slide. These magazines are carried in a caisson of which the following is an illustration:

In this caisson there are from 10 to 20 sets of magazines fully charged. Each set contains 240 to 480 rounds, according to length of magazine, and the gun may be fired at the rate of 60 broadsides, or 720 shots in a minute! A hand-battery of this kind, caliber 50 to 75, would weigh 800 to 1,000 pounds, and can, therefore, be easily handled by the men. Only *one man* is needed to work this battery, and, as the foregoing illustration will show, he is well protected from the shots of the enemy.

In the engraving on page 147, the battery has been halted upon a hill commanding the enemy upon another hill, at a distance presumably of one or more miles. The men are observed drawing a set of loaded magazines from the caisson, which, at the word, they will fit into place on the battery, removing the empty set very quickly. So rapidly can this be done that the cessation of firing is hardly apparent.

BATTERY GUNS.

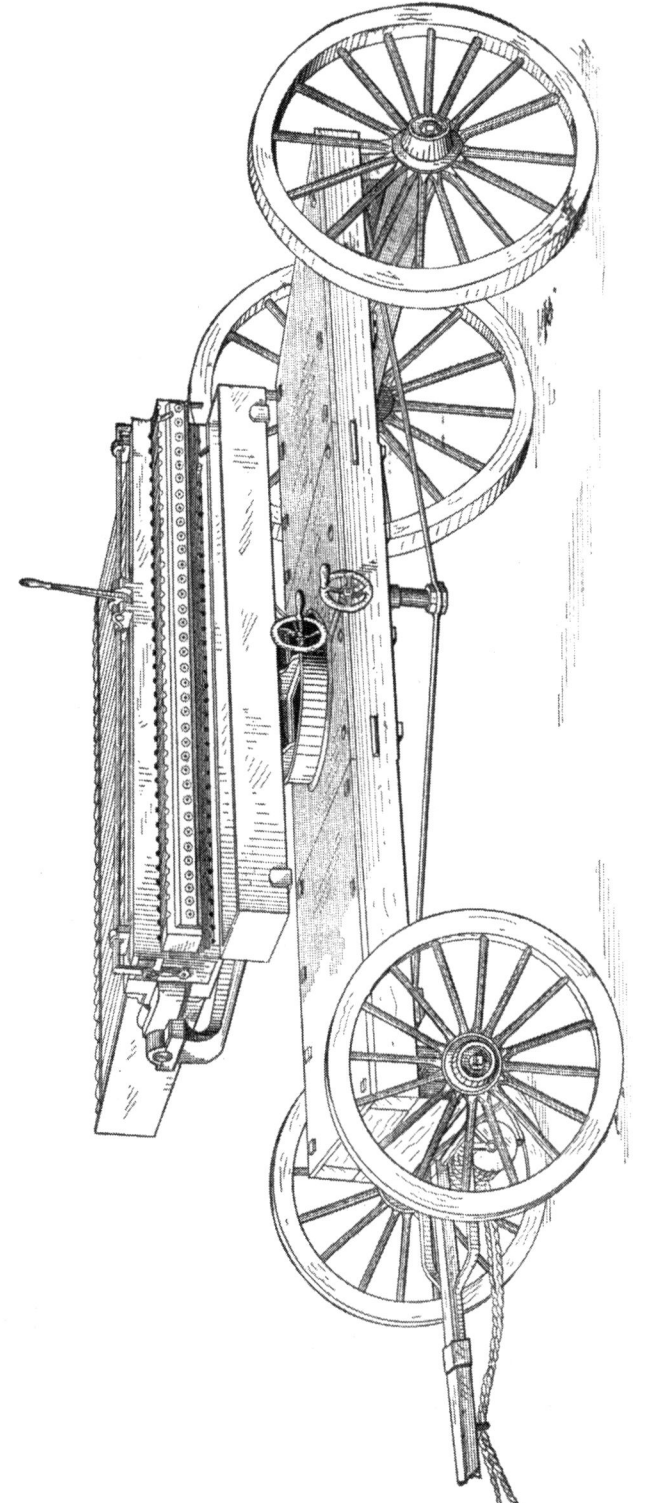

The Perfection of Magazine Battery Guns—The "Lady McLean"—Capable of throwing 1,584 to 2,000 Shots in a Minute!
(Perspective View.)

Never let it be forgotten that the old gun-barrels of all nations can be used in the manufacture of these terrible and formidable batteries!

THE LADY McLEAN.

We claim that this battery is the perfection of magazine ordnance, it is named in honor of Dr. McLean's wife, Lady McLean.

The opposite engraving illustrates the *perfection* of battery guns. It has 36 barrels and 72 magazines. Each magazine will contain 22 charges or more, hence the gun, fully loaded, is capable of throwing 44 broadsides of 36 shots each, or 1,584 or 2,000 shots in the space of *less than one minute!* and this terrible work requires only ONE MAN to do it.

A CHALLENGE TO THE WORLD!

Dr. J. H. McLean distinctly challenges the inventors of all nations to produce any kind of a battery gun that will excel, or even equal, this performance. The "Lady McLean" hand-battery is mounted on a light-running gear, as is seen in the engraving, and weighs from 800 to 1,200 pounds, 50 to 75 caliber, and is a deadly and dreadful weapon at one mile or more range. It can be fired in any position, wheeled entirely around, depressed and elevated at will, and fired rapidly by a single operator all of the time. It has no ungainly hopper to obstruct its accuracy of aim, and its barrels being ranged in a perfectly parallel line, it sweeps a circle by moving its wheel, and cuts like a great sabre. A line of these batteries will do much greater execution than a line of men holding the same number of rifles, because every rifle of a battle-line is separately aimed; but the 36 ponderous rifles in each of these terrible guns has a single eye to direct them, and uses a telescopic sight, and there is no flinching when the trigger is pulled! The whole 36 shots go crashing like a giant's sabre, and cut down whole ranks at a sweep.

One reason why the old battery guns have not won more public favor is,

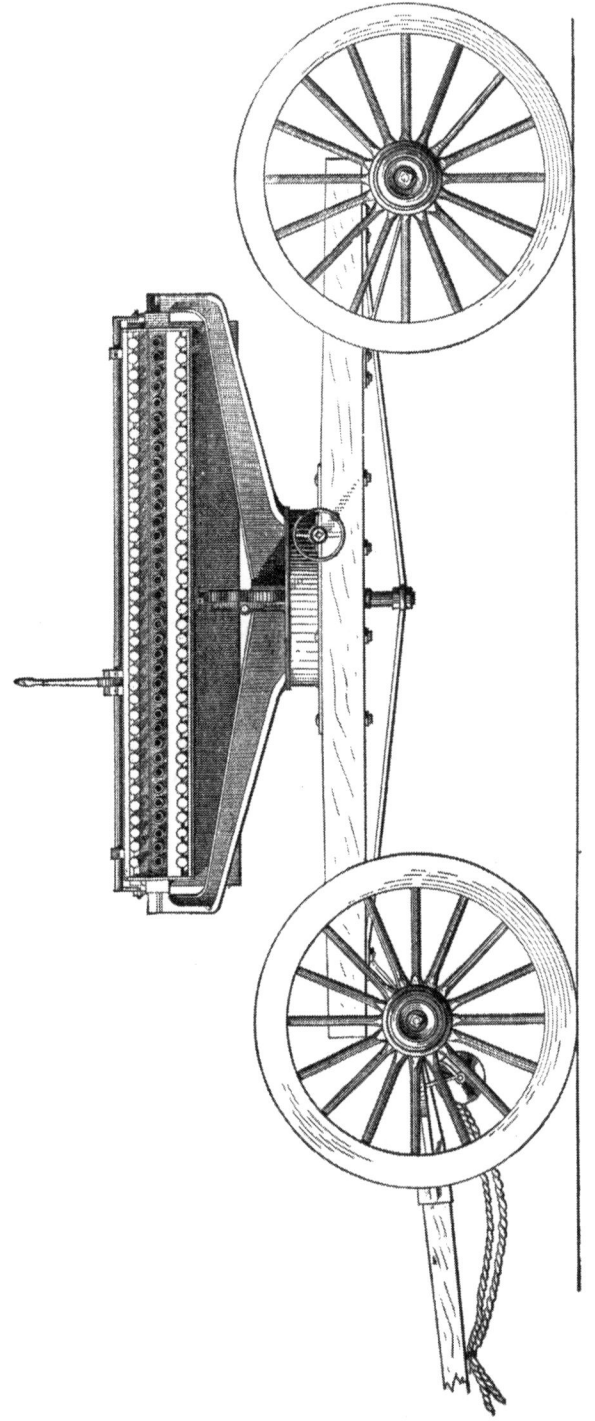

The "Lady McLean" Magazine Battery Gun. (Elevation.)

that they have been made too light, and in thick woods or on brushy battle-fields they cannot be used with any kind of effect.

But Dr. J. H. McLean's battery guns are free from this objection. They are made 75 and 150 caliber. The lightest calibers are intended to be used in all lines of battle, and can be easily handled by infantry. The largest have a range of two to three miles, and are intended to replace cannon entirely, except where breaches in thick walls are to be made.

DESTRUCTIVE CHARACTER OF THESE BATTERIES.

Nothing more terrible can be conceived than the destruction which can be produced by a line of "Lady McLean Horse-Batteries." The illustration opposite is a faint picture of what would follow a "charge of the light brigade," upon a line of these dreadful guns. Their annihilating broadsides can be delivered as rapidly as the gunner can shove the lever back and forth, and they can shoot 3-pound shells quite as well as solid shots, 36 at every broadside, and 44 broadsides in less than one minute.

It would be folly, *madness*, to charge a line of such guns, and their long range and weight of ball makes them available instead of cannon.

BRUSH AND TREES MOWED DOWN!

These guns can be used in the woods effectually, no matter how thick the undergrowth is, for with every broadside the ground would be mowed clean. Quite large trees would be cut down instantly, and the small trash would melt as grass before a horse-reaper. Just think of 36 balls of five pounds weight issuing out of 36 compact steel barrels all in line! Nothing could stand before such a crash! Men and animals of all kinds would go suddenly down in death together, as is illustrated in the engraving opposite.

Charge of the "Light Brigade" on a Line of "Lady McLean" Battery Guns.

Dr. J. H. McLean's Battery Gun "Lady McLean" Going into Action.

THESE BATTERIES AGAINST THE WORLD!

The world has never had a weapon of this terrific character before, and Dr. J. H. McLean challenges all inventors to produce one that will excel it. Dr. McLean is ready to match his hand-battery "Lady McLean," and one man against thirty-six of the best rifle shots the world can produce. The conditions being these: The thirty-six riflemen to choose their distance, and in a body spend five minutes in firing at a line of targets. The Doctor will then produce his battery gun and one man, and, from the same distance, fire five minutes on the same line of targets. The result of the shooting shall determine which would have been most fatal to a line of living men. Surely, no proposition could be fairer. Dr. J. H. McLean claims that his one man will fire more shots and do greater execution than the thirty-six men will; and that, supposing the enemy were returning the fire, a number of the thirty-six men would be killed, whereas his one man stands in comparative safety behind his gun.

At all events, in actual engagements, he will be exposing but *one man at a time, and do more fatal firing than thirty-six fully exposed men can do.* Yes, or even a THOUSAND men; because his one man will direct the thirty-six guns with a telescopic sight, and shoot further, more rapidly and more accurately than the thirty-six possibly can.

MAGAZINE SMALL ARMS.

MAGAZINE, or repeating rifles, have been manufactured for many years, and have been brought into use, to a greater or less extent, in all the principal nations and quarters of the globe. Even the savages of all continents have acquired a few of them, and become proportionately defiant and troublesome to aggressors, as General CUSTER and Major THORNBURG have learned to their cost.

WHAT CONSTITUTES A MAGAZINE GUN.

A magazine gun is one which is provided with tubes parallel with the barrel, or with chambers in the breech, for storing a quantity of cartridges, which can be projected into firing position with one or more movements of a lever connected with the weapon. In revolving arms this lever is sometimes the hammer and sometimes the trigger. In tube and chambered magazines, it is the trigger guard that is used, but in all cases a movement of some kind is necessary to remove the empty shell and bring the cartridge into firing position.

The magazine rifle, most simple in its construction, and capable of storing up for use the greatest number of shots, will, finally, be the one that will crowd out and replace all others.

Dr. McLEAN'S REPEATER AGAINST THE WORLD!

It is believed that Dr. J. H. McLEAN's Repeating Rifle will prove to be the long looked for and universally used weapon:

1st. Because it can be manufactured cheaper than any other.

2d. Because it has a reserve of from 32 to 128 cartridges, as required.

3d. Because it is simplicity itself, and may be worked by the dullest person,

4th. Because it can be fired with *double the rapidity of any existing rifle*, if necessary, and the entire 128 shots can be delivered without removing the gun from the shoulder.

5th. Because it is furnished with an elastic breech, and does not "kick."

6th. Because it is self-cocking.

7th. Because, by a single movement of its slide, it is rendered perfectly harmless in the hands of a child or other inexperienced person, making it absolutely safe to handle.

8th. Because all the old-fashioned rifle barrels in the world can be easily and cheaply converted into these wonderful guns. ☞ Remember this fact.

HOW THESE PEACE-MAKERS LOOK.

When any invention becomes celebrated or has unusually meritorious points, there is a universal desire to see how the thing looks. Realizing this fact, Dr. McLean has spared no expense to inform the reader by illustration, as well as by description, what his wonderful Peace-Makers look like. The following is a cut of the most formidable shoulder gun ever invented. It has a circle of eight magazines around the barrel, each of which may be made to hold 16 charges, so that the rifle, when fully charged, is capable of delivering 128 shots with whatever rapidity the operator may choose, for he has only to pull the trigger, all the other movements of the piece being automatic and resulting from the force of the discharge.

The Dr. J. H. McLean 128 Shot Magazine Rifle "James Gordon Bennett."

THIS RIFLE NO HEAVIER THAN OTHER RIFLES.

When any one, not fully "up" in rifle experience, is told that there is a rifle which carries 128 rounds of ammunition in its magazines, the first conclusion reached would be that such a weapon would be too heavy and cumbersome to carry. Such, however, is not the fact, and any one familiar with rifle shooting or general sporting with fire-arms will know that all rifles are made of a certain weight, from 10 to 14 pounds, to prevent too much recoil and insure accuracy. If a rifle of 45 calibre, using 70 grains of powder and 420 grains of lead, is made lighter than 10 pounds, it will kick badly, but if this amount of weight is in the piece somewhere, that is sufficient.

The Dr. J. H. McLean Magazine Shoulder Guns are all provided with a rubber recoil cushion which absorbs a large percentage of the recoil and enables the barrel of the rifle to be 5 pounds lighter than the ordinary target rifle. This 5 pounds may be taken up in part by the magazines and cartridges; therefore, the wonderful shoulder guns projected by Dr. McLean are, in reality, lighter than any rifle now in existence.

The 64 Shot Rifle.

The above cut shows the 64 shot rifle. It has 4 magazines, 2 on each side, one over the other, each holding 16 shots. This rifle, fully charged, need not weigh more than 8½ to 9 pounds, and every rifle of the standard government calibre ought to weigh that much. If it is lighter, no very good shooting need be expected. Yet it must be continually borne in mind that each of these

WONDERFUL SHOULDER GUNS,

projected by Dr. McLean, is provided with a recoil cushion that takes up so large a percentage of the "kick" as to make a light gun as steady as one of the heavier ones which are now in common use.

The 32 Shot Rifle.

The rifle shown in the above illustration has but two magazines, one on each side, each containing 16 charges; hence, this rifle will carry but 32 charges.

It is, however, 100 per cent. better, in this respect, than any magazine rifle now manufactured. This weapon will be manufactured, most probably, to weigh 7 lbs., and it will be the lightest and most formidable rifle ever put into the hands of man.

THE GREAT WEAPON FOR THE HUNTER.

If a hunter desires to take numerous charges of powder and ball with him he cannot have them any lighter in one shape than another, and *in no other way* can they be made so handy to use and so convenient to carry, as to put them into the magazines of his rifle.

With 32 to 128 charges in his rifle the hunter is always ready for emergencies of any kind. He has but to aim his gun and pull trigger, for it is self-cocking, and the trigger is the lever which loads the piece from the magazines.

If a dozen grizzlies assailed him in a body, he need not flinch, for he has the lives of one hundred and twenty-eight at his fingers' ends. A traveler in the black forests of Russia, armed with one of these formidable rifles, could

LAUGH THE WOLVES TO SCORN;

for, by the time he had laid 128 of them low, a panic would seize all the remainder of the rapacious pack, no matter what were its extent.

To the buffalo hunter, mounted upon a fleet horse, the 128 shot repeater would be a perfect treasure; and, in fact, there is scarcely a situation where more than a single shot is required where this unparalleled gun would not be appreciated as it deserves.

It will shoot just as far and just as true as any other rifle, while for rapidity of firing and number of shots held in reserve, it is without an equal in the world.

The "Hunter's Last Shot" is a work of art which has been much admired; but if the aforesaid hunter had been armed with one of Dr. J. H. McLean's 128 shot repeaters, as the foregoing one is supposed to be, it would not have been his "last shot" by a jug full. Long before he had expended half of the contents of his repeater, the cautious red men would have given him up as game too risky to pursue.

Think of the valuable lives that might have been saved had the soldiers under Thornburg and Custer been armed with such rifles as the above. Then, provided with Dr. J. H. McLean's iron forms, for fortifications, every handful of soldiers on the plains becomes thoroughly impregnable. It would be but the work of an instant for the forms to be unloaded and set for fortifications, and from behind the first line of them so set, the rifles of a few could cover and protect those still at work perfecting an elaborate fort. The world will soon learn to hail Dr. J. H. McLean as its greatest deliverer.

THE GREAT WEAPON FOR THE ARMY.

That Dr. J. H. McLean's wonderful magazine rifles are the only weapons for the soldiers of all nations, there ought not to be two opinions. It need not be feared that these guns will increase the expenditure of ammunition. On the contrary, Dr. McLean distinctly takes the opposite view, and declares it as his opinion that much less ammunition will be expended in a battle, in proportion to

THE HAVOC CREATED,

than is spent with either the old muzzle-loaders or the simple single breech-loaders, now so extensively used; and the reason why, is, that when a soldier is conscious that he has but to crook his finger to discharge his piece; that he need not stop to load; that he is always ready, and complete master of the situation, he loses that nervousness which attacks a man in imminent danger, and who must stop and load, and fear that while so doing an active foe may kill him. Under such circumstances, the average man cannot do good execution. He

Not the "Hunter's Last Shot."

makes haste to load and equal haste to fire. But the soldier lying safely behind one of Dr. J. H. McLean's IRON FORMS, with 128 charges of ammunition in his rifle, ready to be discharged by a single pull of the trigger, fears nothing. If the foe advances he will kill him, no matter what may be the odds against a soldier thus armed and intrenched.

When in action the soldier usually fires as rapidly as he can, with very little regard to the accuracy of his aim. One of the reasons why his aim is mostly too high, and that thousands upon thousands of rounds of ammunition are absolutely wasted, is because, in his nervous haste to fire just as rapidly as he can, he does not take sufficient time to even bring his piece at a "level," much less to take anything like an accurate aim. The loading of his piece, even though it be a breech-loader, requires considerable time, and he is so anxious to be shooting that he pulls trigger as quickly as possible after getting the cartridge in place.

But with the knowledge that his entire 128 cartridges are in readiness to be fired with no motion except to pull the trigger, the nervousness of the soldier would all be gone, and as he is constantly aiming his gun his only care would be to aim accurately. He would fire with much more deliberation than he does where, for a large per cent. of his time, *his gun is unloaded*.

It is, therefore, argued that an army equipped with Dr. J. H. McLean's 128 shot repeaters would do five hundred times greater execution with less ammunition than an army with arms in present use. Hence, it would be more economical to arm soldiers with this weapon, as a small army would effect results greater than large ones now do.

THE OPEN LINE BETTER THAN THE "SHOULDER TO SHOULDER" LINE.

With these arms, sustained by the terribly destructive Lady McLean batteries, and the Annihilating Magazine Cannon, a battle line might be made thin, and safely placed behind the forms, thus making it difficult for the enemy to kill many of the men. Under present arms and tactics the battle line is compact, so as to sustain the shock of charges, and in the belief that the shoulder to shoulder

MAGAZINE SMALL ARMS. 163

Section of Proposed Line of Battle, using the McLean Arms and Iron Forms.

contact imparts a sort of magnetic courage along the entire line. It cannot be denied, however, that rifle balls, grape shot and canister create greater havoc in compact ranks than in skirmish lines, where the men are 10 to 20 feet apart.

Whenever soldiers realize that they have a whole day's fighting in the magazines of their guns, and that no enemy can successfully "charge" their line because of the decimating battery guns stationed along the line, they can be relied on to stand perfectly steady in a long thin line and shoot for hours.

The engraving, page 163, illustrates the safety and impregnability of lines of battle using the McLEAN arms and iron forms.

READY FOR ACTION.

In marching through an enemy's country the soldier must be ready for action at all times, hence he must carry 60 to 100 cartridges. These, put into a belt and hung around his body, are a permanent drag, and when he is permitted to halt and sit down upon the ground for a brief rest, though he may lay down his gun he must not remove his cartridge belt, but with the McLEAN arms he bears no load when his gun is either laid down or rested upon the ground.

Furthermore, it will be found that he can carry the entire 128 rounds placed in the magazines of this gun with much more comfort to himself than he could carry 64 rounds attached around his body, and the added fact that he is constantly prepared to commence a rapid firing, is a heavily preponderating circumstance in favor of the general introduction of Dr. J. H. McLEAN's 128 shot repeating rifle.

How many rounds of ammunition does a soldier take into battle?

One hundred and twenty-eight?

If so, can he get rid of the weight of these charges of powder and ball?

Assuredly not. They are put into a belt and strapped around his waist, and must be carried. Look at the engraving on the following page, of the arms and army of to-day, and compare it with the companion picture of the arms and army of the future, and say which is really the most cumbersome load for the soldier to carry, the heavy rifle and the cartridge belt of to-day, or the 128 shot rifle with no cartridge belt.

The Arms and Army of To-Day.

The Arms and Army of the Future.

IN A TIGHT SPOT.

The history of all wars is replete with anecdotes of persons who have encountered deadly peril and, by some fortunate concatenation of circumstances, escaped without hurt. During the French campaign in Mexico, in 1864, three zouaves got separated from their command and were suddenly attacked by a large body of Mexican lancers. The zouaves were fortunately armed with breech-loaders, and quickly forming a triangle, back to back, they kept at bay the menacing foe until relieved

The illustration, page 168, shows 3 more dangerous men than those described. They are back to back, and are unitedly capable of delivering 384 shots in an incredibly short space of time. Their rifles have an effective range of 1,000 yards, or more, and they could give a fearful account of themselves, though attacked by a thousand cavalry.

Dr. J. H. McLEAN'S MAGAZINE PISTOL.

This formidable pistol is destined to supersede the old-fashioned "revolver" of 5 to 7 shots. Like the 128 shot rifle this pistol has eight magazines arranged around the pistol barrel in a circle, each of which will hold 6 shots, or 48 in all, and they can be delivered as rapidly as the finger can be made to pull the trigger. The annexed cut will give some idea of the appearance of these extraordinary weapons.

The 48 Shot Pistol.

A Dangerous Trio.

The engraving, page 170, shows what a hunted and desperate dragoon armed with a brace of Dr. J. H. McLean's repeating pistols can be expected to do. These pistols carry 48 shots each, hence this resolute man has possibly the lives of 96 of his would-be captors at will. At all events, he might prove a very ugly customer to deal with. Old rifle barrels of 32 to 45 calibre, if sound, can be cut up and converted into these repeating pistols, and by this means every nation can put itself upon a splendid war footing for a moderate sum of money.

A CHALLENGE TO THE WORLD.

Dr. J. H. McLean challenges every other repeating rifle in existence to public trial, test to be as follows:

Greatest number of shots fired in ten minutes; accuracy and execution considered.

Distance, weight of charge; size of target to be same in all cases.

THE GREAT SPORTING GUN OF THE WORLD.

Dr. J. H. McLean herewith presents an illustration of his wonderful rifled magazine shot gun, destined to become the great sporting gun of the world:

McLean's Rifled Magazine Shot Gun "Bogardus."—(Top View.)

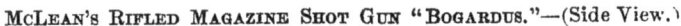

McLean's Rifled Magazine Shot Gun "Bogardus."—(Side View.)

This is the perfection of fowling pieces, all charges being delivered through the central barrel, making it unnecessary to shift the aim from the right to the left barrel, as in the ordinary double-barreled gun. The cartridges for this hunting gun are so manufactured as to "take the grooves" and impart a rotary motion to the charge, which causes it to cover the game close and evenly. This gun is

170 *Dr. J. H. McLEAN'S PEACE-MAKERS.*

AN UGLY CUSTOMER.

to be furnished with from 2 to 4 magazines, as desired, and will contain about 48 to 50 rounds. In hunting where large game is likely to be met with, ball cartridges should be placed in the lower magazines, and then, by a quick push of a lever, they can be used instead of the shot cartridges.

☞ There are fortunes to be made in the manufacture of this great sporting gun.

FORTUNES TO BE MADE EVERYWHERE.

The important fact that companies formed in each nation for the manufacture of Dr. J. H. McLean's Peace-Makers can contract with their governments to convert all sound old-fashioned guns into these formidable repeaters at a great saving to the government must be steadily remembered. In this business alone companies can make fortunes in each nation. Address Dr. J. H. McLean, 314 Chestnut street, St. Louis, Mo.

TORPEDOES.

The Torpedo is the master of the mightiest frigate, armored or unarmored, and even in its present undeveloped condition is a terror to every navy. There are many kinds of torpedoes, from the inexpensive jug filled with gunpowder and fitted up, through the cork, with a primer, to those electrical machines costing many thousands of dollars, and yet which have so far failed to inspire any government with faith in their effectiveness. It is perfectly safe to say that, up to the present moment, no torpedo has been invented which may be implicitly relied upon to do the work wanted of it every time. It is said that when the commander of the Peruvian frigate Huascar tried to send one of the "Whitehead" torpedoes to blow up the enemy's vessel, the extraordinary spectacle of the torpedo turning completely around in the water, and swimming back to the Huascar, was witnessed by the astonished crew, and, but for the fact that one of the officers jumped into the water and steered the dangerous missive aside, the Peruvians would have been incontinently hoisted by their own petard. It is plain enough that that sort of conduct in a torpedo *won't do.*

WHAT CONSTITUTES AN EFFECTIVE TORPEDO.

To be effective, it has been found that a torpedo must be made to go to the ship, instead of expecting the ship to come to the torpedo.

Not only must the torpedo go to the ship and stay there until exploded, but it must be certain to explode at a sufficient depth below the surface, to insure the destruction of the vessel against which it is dispatched.

Not only this, but the torpedo which will receive the confidence of all governments, must be able to make its way to the ship despite any and every effort of those in command of the ship to the contrary.

THE BUSINESS OF A SHIP WHEN THE APPROACH OF TORPEDOES IS SUSPECTED.

It is the business of the ship to prevent the approach of the torpedo, and when the commander is fully aware that it is the intention of his enemy to send a torpedo against his vessel, he may frustrate that intention by moving out of the way, by bombarding his enemy, or by capturing the torpedo; all depending, of course, on the kind of torpedo to be sent and the method employed in sending it.

If it is a torpedo to be guided by wires from a torpedo boat, and fired by electricity when it has reached the vessel against which it is directed, the commander of that vessel may easily prevent the execution of the design by moving off, or may throw out boats-crews to cut the connection between the torpedo and the torpedo boat before the torpedo reaches his vessel, and while his boats are out on this mission, he may open a severe fire on the torpedo boat.

The severing of the connection between the torpedo and the torpedo boat removes all danger from the torpedo, which may then be allowed to sink, or may be safely captured.

If a percussion torpedo is used, one that is propelled with a high velocity under the water by compressed air or spring power, and the explosion of which depends upon its striking the vessel with sufficient force to fire one of its fulminates, the vessel against which these are leveled has but little to fear:

First—Because it is almost impossible to make them strike a vessel at all, at any distance from their point of departure. Distance, strong currents, and the retarding influence of the water, all conspire to prevent.

Second—A netting or crinoline around the ship is sure protection against them.

Third—The ship may keep moving about when the intention of the enemy is discovered, and may also open fire on the torpedo launch, for in order that such torpedoes be made at all effective, they must be dropped in the water within a few hundred yards of the ship to be assailed.

Fourth — If the torpedo is propelled by a compressed air motor, there will be a line of bubbles on the surface of the water, showing the exact course of the torpedo and its speed, by which means it may be avoided.

THE TORPEDOES OF THE FUTURE.

Having succinctly described what the torpedo of the future *must be*, in order to insure confidence, it will very naturally be asked, where can such a torpedo be found ? It can be found among the terrible Magnetic Torpedoes now offered to the world by Dr. J. H. McLean, of St. Louis, Mo.

First—The Dr. J. H. McLean Torpedoes cannot be avoided.

Second—They will be easily sent to the ship, they will stay there, and they will do their work surely and well after arriving there.

They are of two kinds, the submarine and the projectile.

The following illustration will give the reader a fair idea of the outward appearance of the submarine torpedoes:

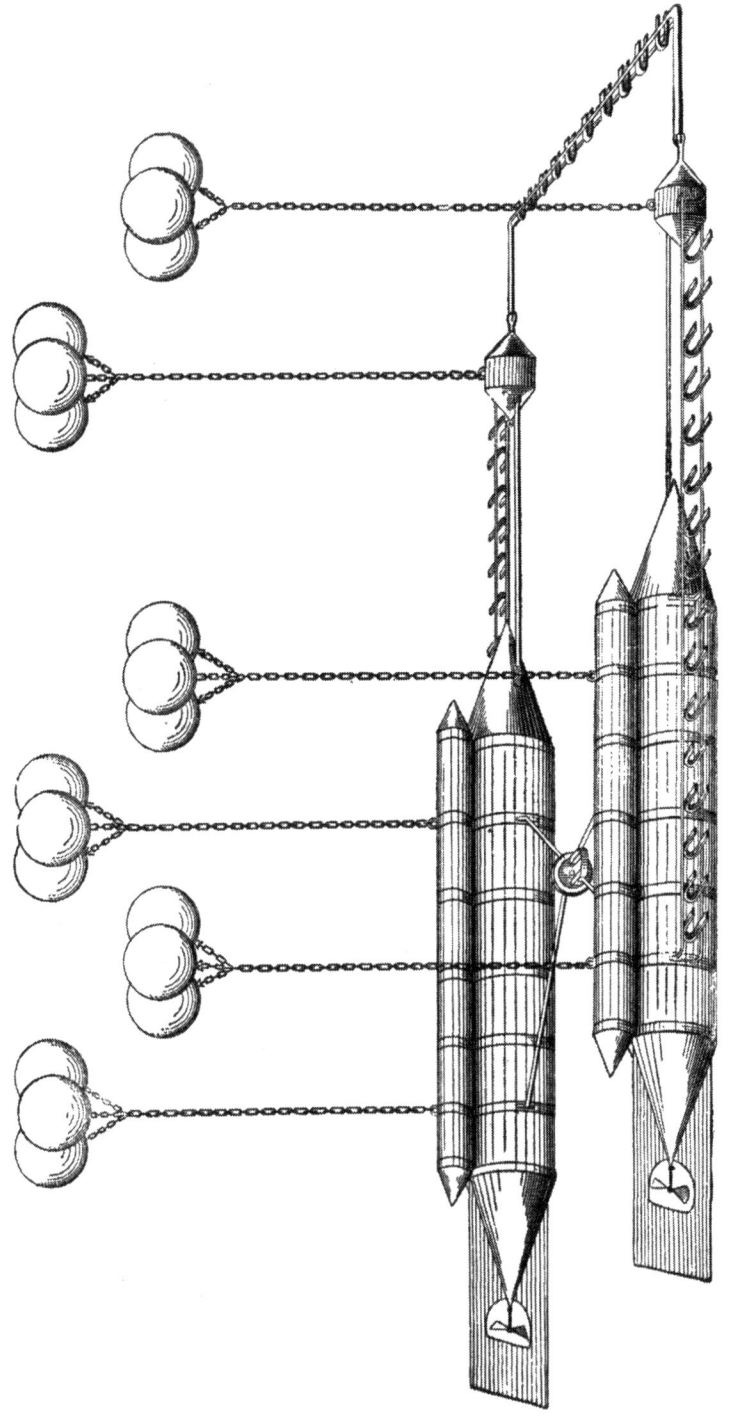

Dr. J. H. McLean's "Octopus" or "Devil-Fish" Torpedo.—(Double.)

These torpedoes are called "Octopus" or Devil-Fish torpedoes, on account of the fact that they attach themselves firmly to the side of the ship, and remain thus attached until the firing mechanism inside of the torpedo explodes the nitro-glycerine with which it is charged, and the ship is destroyed. It is easily seen that there are numerous *horse-shoe magnets* used to attach these torpedoes to the vessel against which they are directed.

It is presumed no intelligent person will doubt the fact of such adherence, once the torpedo arrives at the vessel.

Very good. The means of propelling the torpedo are ample. It can be directed from a plain schooner miles away, and it will not miss its prey.

Besides, the schooner may lower half-a-dozen of them into the water, and direct them from various angles against the unsuspecting vessel or vessels.

They approach slowly. It will take 2 hours to send them to the vessel from a schooner 6 miles away, and entirely out of danger of the ship's guns.

They give no surface indication of their approach. They do not strike the ship with any force, and if the far-away schooner had been suspected of launching such torpedoes, the long time elapsing before the torpedo arrives and gets in its work would lull all suspicion.

Besides, if the vessel moves to avoid one, she may only attract another one to her iron sides in the direction which she is going, for they are cheap to build, and the schooner may waste a hundred of them economically in destroying one iron clad.

They can be sent singly or in pairs, as the following cuts will illustrate.

The long cigar-shaped part is the boat of the torpedo, containing the motive power.

The diamond-shaped vessels on the ends of the long rods are the torpedoes, charged with one hundred pounds of a preparation of nitro-glycerine, having twelve times the explosive energy of the best prismatic gunpowder.

TORPEDOES.

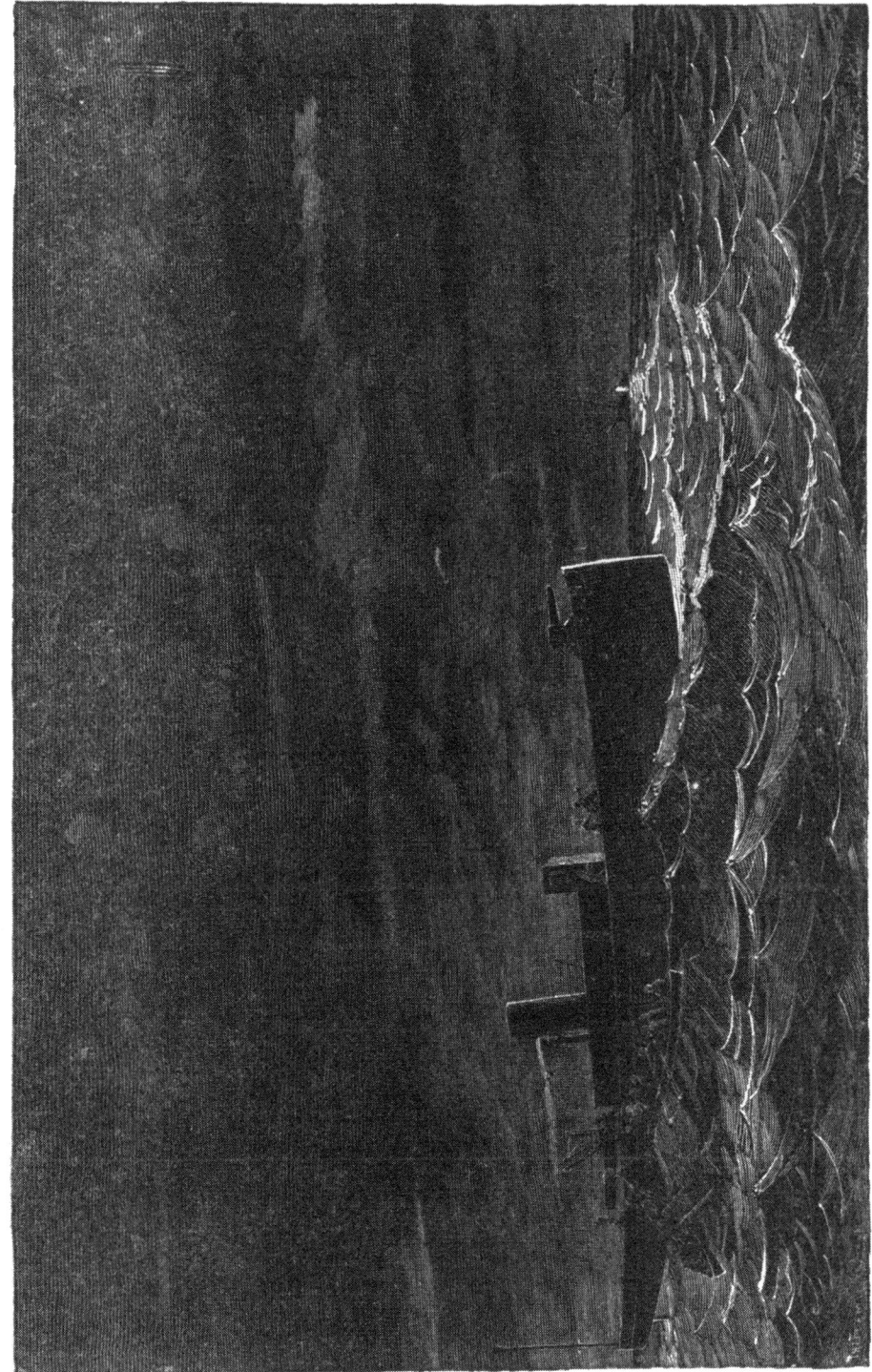

Destroying Blockades at Night with Dr. J. H. McLean's "Octopus" or "Devil-Fish" Torpedoes.

THE FIRING MECHANISM.

It is shown above that Dr. McLean sends his torpedo to the vessel, and provides powerful magnets to attract it toward the iron ship, when it comes near to it, and hold it there indefinitely after it makes itself fast. It now remains to be shown how the Doctor explodes his torpedo after it becomes fastened to the vessel.

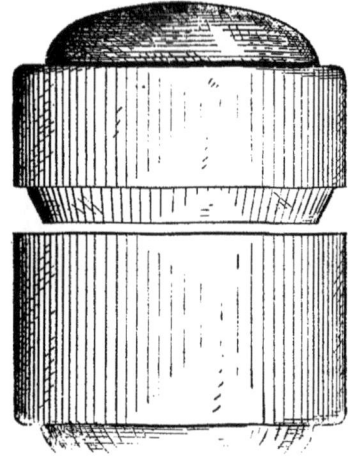

RUBBER COVER FOR THE FIRING MECHANISM.

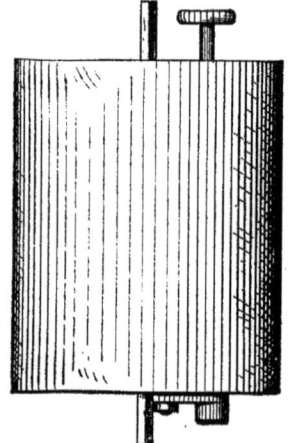

THE FIRING MECHANISM.

Inside of this torpedo the above ingenious mechanism is placed, and it will fire a rifle cartridge of powder into the nitro-glycerine preparation of the torpedo at the exact time required.

Suppose the distance for the torpedo to travel is six miles. It moves only three miles per hour, therefore it will take two hours to reach the ship. The mechanism is set to explode in three hours. This gives ample time for miscalculation of distance.

Suppose the commander of the ship really suspects the far-away schooner is dropping torpedoes directly against his vessel, and orders out numerous boats to fish for them.

They find one, and naturally hoist it on deck; if not, what shall they do with it?

If they do hoist it on deck, it will be the dearest capture that ship ever made; for, at the appointed time, the firing mechanism will fire the awful charge in the torpedo, and the ship would be a wreck.

But more than one torpedo will always be launched against a vessel, and it is scarcely possible that they could all be captured, as they cannot be seen, and there is no way of ascertaining their whereabouts, for they are in constant motion, though the motion is slow.

These submarine torpedoes are solely designed for the destruction of blockading vessels—iron-clads; for iron-clad rams would make short work with unarmored blockaders, thus rendering the work of torpedoes unnecessary.

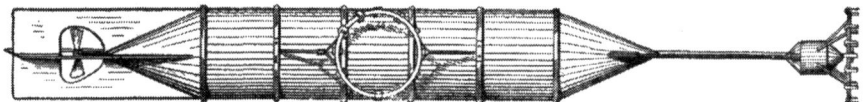

Dr. J. H. McLean's "Octopus" or "Devil-Fish" Torpedo.—(Single.)

The above illustration exhibits the single "Octopus." Like the double octopus, it is provided with powerful magnets to guide it toward the ship when it reaches the vicinity of one, and to firmly attach itself to the ship, so that it may remain there until the firing mechanism, with which it is also provided, gets in its work.

THE MOST TERRIBLE OF ALL TORPEDOES, THE "THUNDERBOLT!"

The following illustration exhibits a still more terrible weapon—Dr. J. H. McLean's Projectile Torpedo, the "Thunderbolt."

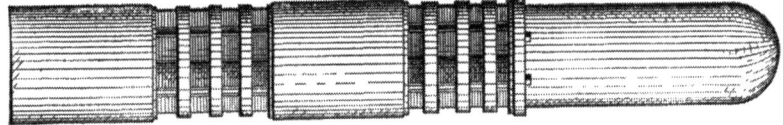

Dr. J. H. McLean's Projectile Torpedo "Thunderbolt."

This is a torpedo designed to be thrown from a cannon—eight inch, ten inch, or fifteen inches diameter, as the case may be. The entire bolt is hollow and made water-tight. The lower or torpedo end is the heaviest, enough the heaviest to keep the bolt from "tumbling" when fired. When fired from one of Dr. McLean's Hercules Guns, a device to compel it to "take the groove" of the gun has been invented, and thus carry it steadily through the air and drop it exactly where desired. There are several zones of horse-shoe magnets around the torpedo, with the poles pointing outward.

The torpedo end is charged with one hundred pounds of the same preparation used in the submarine torpedoes, and supplied with a similar mechanism for firing the charge.

This preparation of nitro-glycerine is one just patented, and will not explode by concussion, but explodes very readily by having powder fired into it.

These torpedoes may be used with certain effect by forts or land batteries against vessels attacking them, or by iron-clad torpedo boats carrying one or two large guns.

The weight of this torpedo is calculated to be enough, less than the water it displaces when thrown into the sea, to insure its rising toward the surface after its submersion consequent upon its plunge into the water from the cannon. If near the ship, as it rises, the magnets will be attracted by the ship's armor, and it will cling to it until the mechanism inside the torpedo fires it and destroys the ship.

Naturally the firing time of the mechanisms used in these torpedoes would not exceed five to twenty minutes, and if the vessels attacked were moving about they would all of the time be liable to pick up one of these torpedoes where many were thrown.

These are very inexpensive torpedoes, and may be used as freely as so many shells of like calibre.

AN OFFER TO ALL GOVERNMENTS.

Dr. J. H. McLean hereby agrees to enter into a good and sufficient bond with any government desiring to build and try these torpedoes, that they can be made to destroy vessels, as described, if built under the superintendence of persons whom the Doctor shall name.

THE DESTROYER OF THE WORLD'S NAVIES.—WILL THE NATIONS KEEP THE PEACE?

If experiments substantiate the Doctor's position—as surely will be the case—then one immense stride is taken toward compelling all nations to keep the peace.

What becomes of any nation's power at sea in face of so sure and cheap a means of destroying their most formidable vessels? And without power at sea, the influence of one or two powerful governments, that might be named, is dwarfed to insignificance.

Russia has ordered a new iron-clad ship to be built in England, which, for strength and invulnerability of armor, surpasses all previous efforts. But the *London Times* says, "this monster vessel, like the meanest of its class, must take its chance with the 'coming torpedo.'"

That torpedo has come.

DR. J. H. McLEAN'S ROCKET TORPEDOES.

Dr. McLean recognizes the fact that torpedo attack is yet in its infancy, and the further fact that torpedoes are eventually to become the annihilators of iron-clad ships, as now constructed, hence he has made torpedoes a pretty thorough study.

In the foregoing articles he has described some torpedoes which he regards as infallible, and it might be supposed he would be content to rest there. But Dr. McLean delights in covering every inch of a subject when he begins to investigate, and to show how carefully he has gone over the subject of torpedoes, he submits the following drawings and descriptions of what may also prove to be a formidable and infallible torpedo:

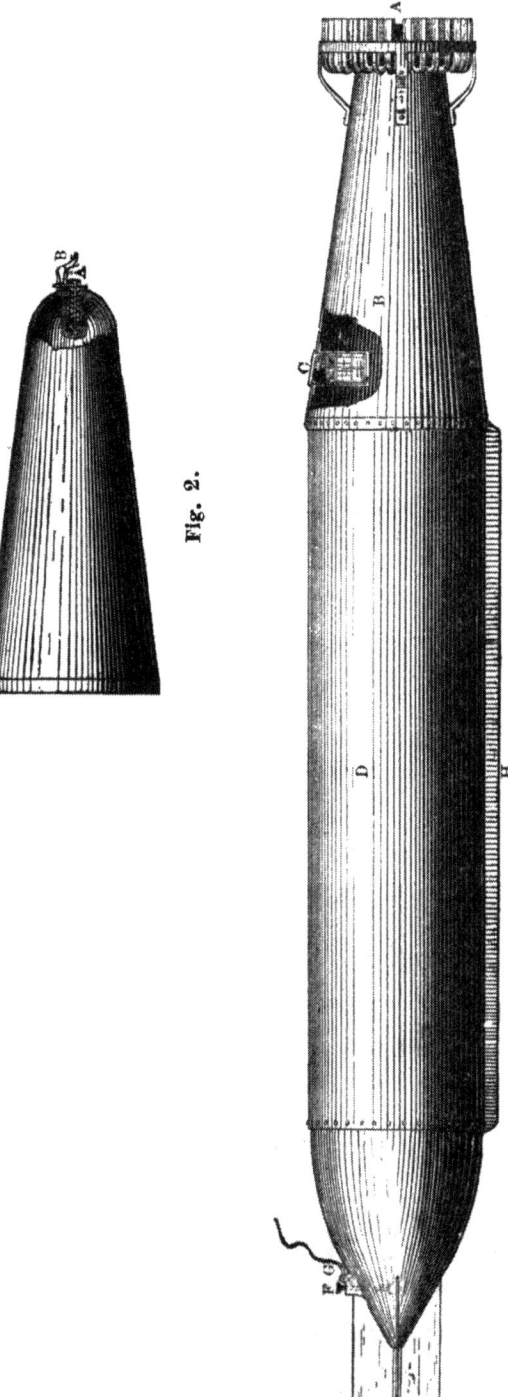

Fig. 2.

DR. J. H. MCLEAN'S SUBMARINE ROCKET TORPEDO.

A.—Horse-shoe magnets to attach and hold it to the vessel.
B.—Receptacle of the explosive compound.
C.—Time-firing mechanism, enveloped in its rubber case.
D.—Air chamber cylinder.
E.—Vent through which the rocket powder will escape after being ignited, and by its pressure against the water force the torpedo along.
F.—Percussion lock for firing the propelling powder after the torpedo is lowered into position.
G.—Lanyard attached to the percussion lock.
H.—Keel of the torpedo.

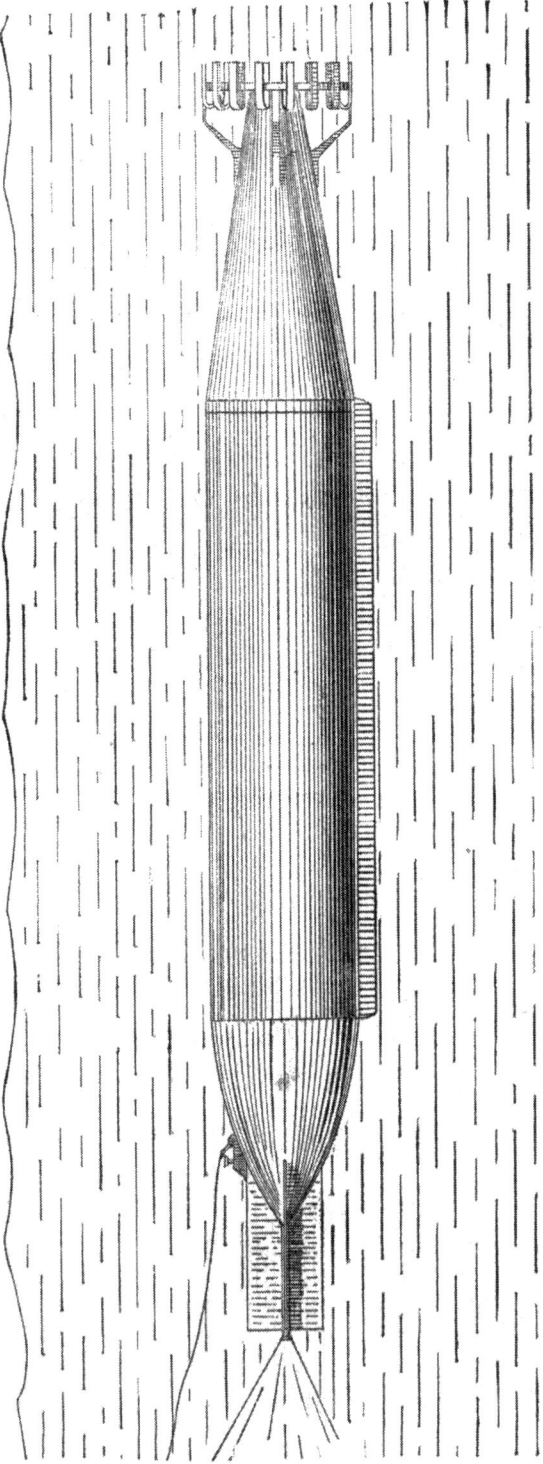

Dr. J. H. McLean's Submarine Rocket Torpedo as it would appear Moving beneath the Water.

A and B, in first engraving, show the percussion lock arranged upon the front end of the torpedo, so that the explosion may take place immediately upon the contact of the torpedo with the ship. In such torpedoes the time-firing mechanism would not be used.

The second cut illustrates the submarine torpedo moving through the water.

The rocket powder shown to be ignited, the flame of which is seen issuing from the rear of the torpedo, is contained in an inner tube running directly through the center of the air chamber. While this powder is burning, the torpedo must necessarily be driven through the water with great rapidity, and it will go pretty straight in the line of its direction. Let us suppose it reaches the ship. Its position on first contact, and its subsequent position, are illustrated by the following diagram:

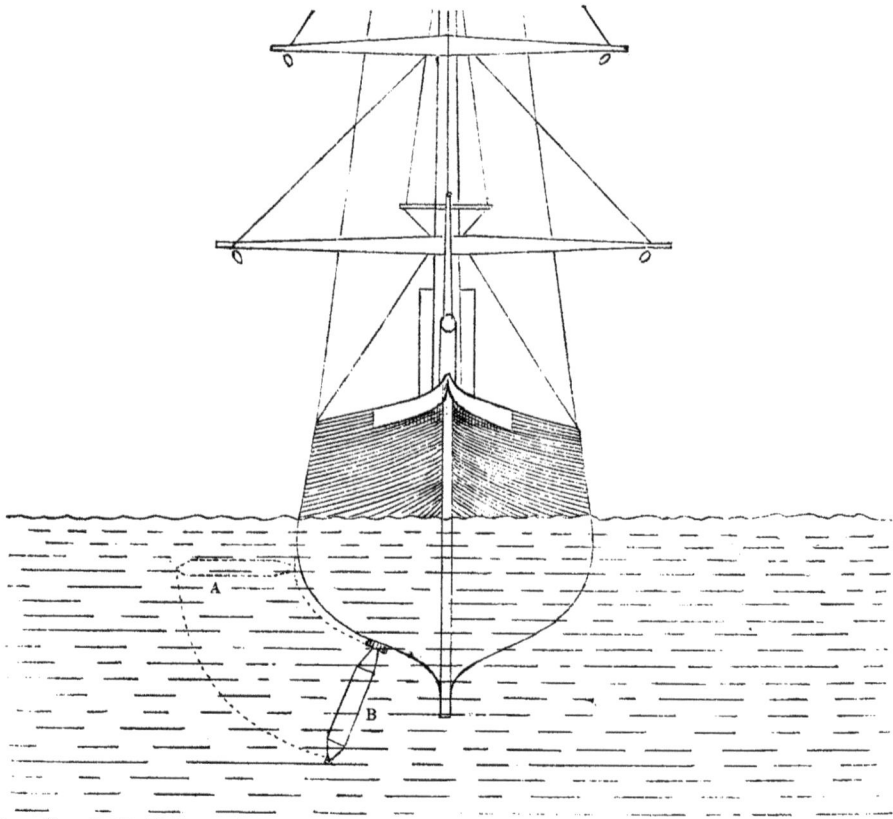

THE DR. J. H. McLEAN SUBMARINE ROCKET TORPEDO ARRIVES AT THE SHIP AND SWINGS AROUND UNDER ITS BOTTOM.

A.—Position of Torpedo on contact.   B.—Final Position.

When the torpedo above described is lowered into the water to be directed against a ship, it is proposed to lower it by means of a well and tubes in the hull of a torpedo boat, to a depth of say 10 feet. If it darts straight forward upon the ship it is aimed at, it would strike the vessel as shown above, and the circle of magnets would take firm hold of the iron armor. As the rocket powder burned out of the tube it would be replaced by water, and the torpedo would then swing downward, but, being held to the ship by the magnets, would slip along down the side of the vessel until directly under her bottom, and then the firing mechanism would explode the torpedo with the following usual effect:

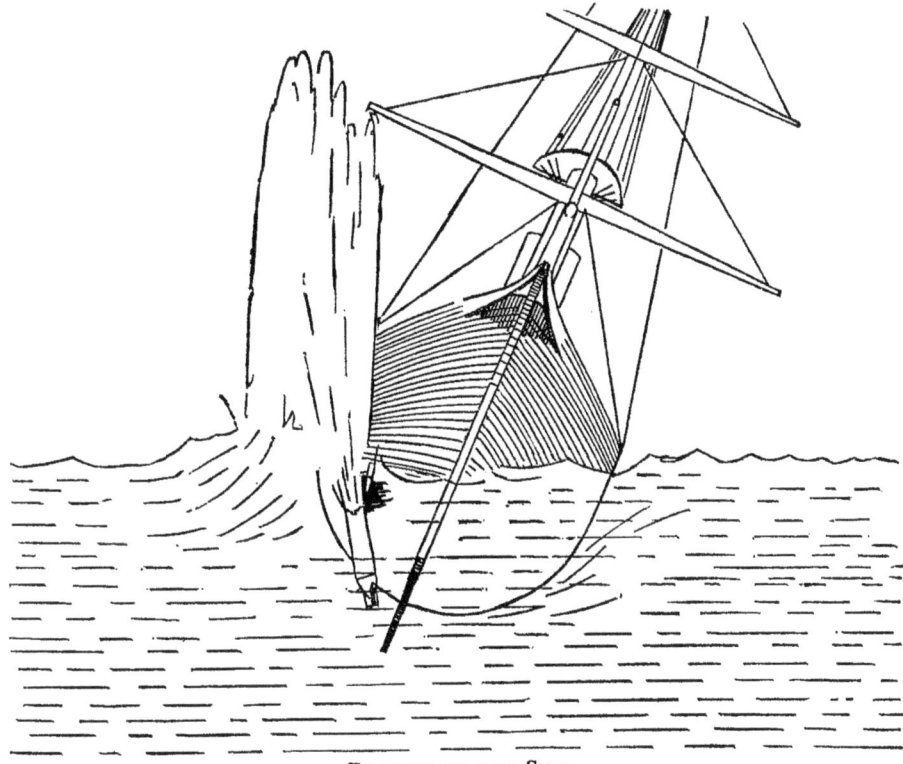

BLOWING UP THE SHIP.

Dr. J. H. McLEAN'S AERIAL ROCKET TORPEDO.

Dr. McLEAN believes that ships in action can be more successfully assailed with torpedoes launched through the air than by those projected under water, and has therefore caused to be invented and presented to the public a rocket

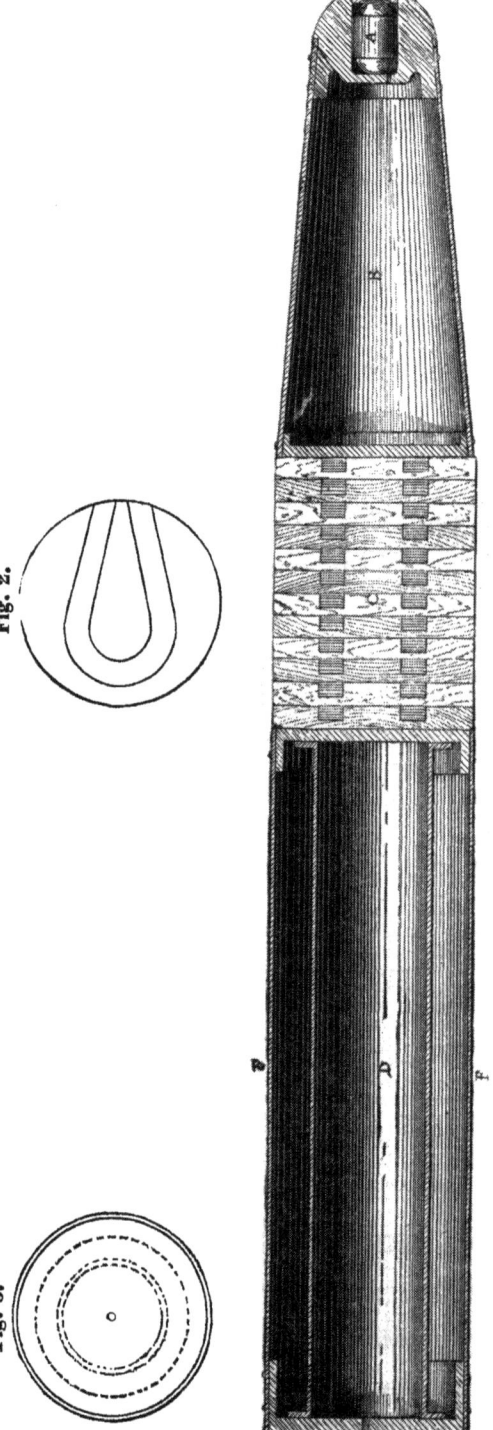

Dr. J. H. McLean's Aerial Rocket Torpedo.

A.—Shows the firing mechanism protected by its rubber envelope.
B.—The receptacle of the explosive compound.
C.—Zone of large, powerful horse-shoe magnets.
D.—Central tube containing the rocket powder.
E.—Vent for same.
F. F.—Air chamber space around the interior tube which contains the rocket powder.
Fig. 2.—Shows a wooden disk with an embedded magnet, used in forming the zone C.
Fig. 3.—Shows the end view of the torpedo.

torpedo to be sent to the vessel through the air. The foregoing illustration exhibits the general appearance of this proposed torpedo.

HOW THESE TORPEDOES ARE TO BE THROWN.

The following diagram exhibits a light wrought-iron howitzer, which Dr. McLean caused to be invented for the purpose of giving direction to these torpedoes:

A.—The rounded end marked by A and the dotted lines, also thus marked, show the position of the torpedo in the howitzer.

B.—Shows the end of a shell which is projected up into the opening of the torpedo cylinder. This shell contains about a pistol charge of powder—say 10 grains.

C.—Percussion lock.

D.—Lanyard.

When the lanyard is pulled, the primer fires the small charge of dry powder directly into the vent of the rocket tube. This ignites the rocket powder and causes the projectile to rise into the air, with ever increasing force and velocity, just as the ordinary rocket does. If the rocket has been well aimed, it drops into the sea near to the vessel, and the magnets attach it to the ship, where it will be firmly held until the firing mechanism does its final work. But even should the shaft have been badly aimed, the rocket is buoyed up in the water with the torpedo end down, and if anywhere near to the vessel, it will be attracted to it by the power of its magnets before the mechanism fires it.

It is believed this Aerial Rocket Torpedo will do splendid work, and, like the other ones described above, it has been patented in all countries granting patents.

The attention of capitalists and of all governments is called to these extraordinary torpedoes.

It has already been shown that Dr. J. H. McLean's Magazine Cannon, terrible battery guns and 128-shot rifles will simply decimate battle lines on land; and now, that his torpedoes will destroy the strongest fleets on the ocean.

It remains to be shown in the next chapter that his time shells are capable of making land fortifications, or earthworks, wholly uninhabitable. No living thing can possibly exist in any inclosed fort as forts are now built.

☞ Companies, for the manufacture of this infallible weapon, ought to be formed in all countries. These torpedoes need not cost more than $100 each, and no government can do without them.

☞ Capitalists wishing further information may address Dr. J. H. McLean, 314 Chestnut street, St. Louis, Mo.

BOMB SHELLS.

BOMB SHELLS are among the most conspicuous munitions of war, and no small amount of brain-power has been expended in the endeavor to produce a shell which should be considered in every way perfect, thus far without notable success. It is probably true, that 30 per cent. of all classes of shells thrown in action, by any army or naval force, fail to explode; and it may be added, with confidence, that at least 30 per cent. of those which do explode, fail of the effect intended, either because the explosion is premature or too long delayed. Shells, as at present constructed, are of two kinds, percussion shells and time shells. By percussion shells is meant those kinds which are fired by coming in contact with a body sufficiently dense to check, in some measure, their progress, causing a detonation of the percussion primers with which they are supplied. By time shells is meant those kinds of shells which are provided either with a fuse or firing-mechanism, which will permit a fixed interval of time to elapse between the projection of the shell and its bursting. The time shells now in common use, all over the world, are provided with a fuse, and, it would be within the facts to state, that not more than 25 per cent. of all such shells thrown in action are ever really effective.

HUNDREDS OF THEM NEVER EXPLODE AT ALL,

hundreds more explode either prematurely or too late to perform the office for which they were thrown, and not a few burst in the guns and seriously damage those who are employed about them. In turning these matters over in his mind, Dr. J. H. McLEAN came to the conclusion that there was wide room for improvement in shells, and with his customary energy and promptness, set at work at once to devise the improvements. The result has been all that could be desired, and Dr. McLean now presents to the world, with pride and confidence, the most successful and dreadfully destructive bomb shells ever constructed.

Dr. J. H. McLean's INCENDIARY TIME SHELL "CYCLONE."

The following illustration shows one of the most destructive shells ever invented:

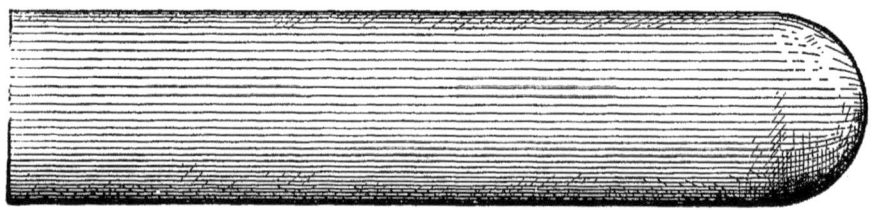

Dr. J. H. McLean's Incendiary Time Shell "Cyclone."

To one who gazes upon this shell nothing of its deadly character is revealed, but a very brief description of it will convince all readers, however lacking they may be in information pertaining to munitions of war, that the "Cyclone" is capable of becoming a most deadly visitant. The one above shown is intended to represent a shell large enough for an eight-inch gun. Such a shell would be eight inches in diameter, and about six diameters in length, or four feet. It would weigh, charged and ready to throw, about 350 lbs., and would require a charge of forty lbs. of powder to drive it to a distance of five miles. In the interior is a bursting charge of ten lbs. of powder, and a large mass of compressed

COTTON SATURATED WITH GASOLINE.

In the forward portion of the shell is fixed, inside of its rubber envelope, and protected by two rubber diaphragms, one of Dr. J. H. McLean's admirable firing mechanisms, illustrations of which have been shown in the preceding article upon torpedoes. This terrible shell is loaded into any eight-inch gun in the ordinary way—through the breech if it be a breech-loader, and through the muzzle if it be a muzzle-loader—and simply fired at the point of attack, the mechanism having been previously set, timed, and inserted. That these fearful shells may create the

GREATEST HAVOC,

it will be better to set the mechanisms so as to explode at irregular intervals, but always allowing time for the "Cyclone" to reach its full destination, and to remain at rest for some period of time, say ten minutes to three hours after it so arrives at its destination. It bears no external evidences of being a shell, but appears rather to be a solid bolt. Suppose, upon shelling a city vigorously for two hours with "Cyclones" the shelling party took a rest. If all of the shells were "set" to explode in two hours from the time the first one was thrown, the enemy would conclude, from the fact that none of the missiles burst, that they were solid bolts, and once having gone crashing through a building, their mischief was over.

During the suspension of the shelling the confident enemy would pour forth from their bomb-proofs and other retreats, and actively resume their varied duties. All of a sudden,

LIKE LIGHTNING FROM A CLEAR SKY,

the dreadful "Cyclones" would commence getting in their horrible work!

Confusion, fire and death, would reign supreme for the next three hours!

The air would vibrate with a constant succession of terrific concussions, and be filled with deadly flying missiles coming from unknown sources, and wild flames would leap up, and thick smoke abound everywhere. Human courage would give way, and a dreadful panic ensue.

THEN THE SHELLING WOULD RECOMMENCE,

and another installment of a thousand or two of these dreadful missiles would be hurled into the devoted city.

With a few hundred of Dr. J. H. McLean's Hercules Guns surrounding a city, no matter how large that city might be, hurling Cyclones into every part of it, its final and complete destruction could only be a question of time, and that time would be exceedingly brief.

Surely, Dr. J. H. McLean's "Cyclone" may be fairly reckoned among his wonderful Peace-Makers, and it is certainly destined to exert its full influence in determining the nations to make war no more.

Notwithstanding the ingenious mechanism with which it is supplied to insure its firing at the desired time, the "Cyclone" will not cost above $1 more than an ordinary shell of equal calibre and weight, and it

WILL NEVER FAIL TO DO ITS WORK,

and it cannot be prematurely exploded, and is therefore perfectly safe to handle. The size of the bursting charge will cause tremendous havoc to buildings into which the Cyclone has forced its way, for that amount of powder will shake down walls, break up foundations, tear off roofs and otherwise demolish all kinds of structures, while the burning cotton will be scattered in all conceivable directions, and cause flames to break out wherever it falls.

Dr. J. H. McLEAN'S TIME SHELL "SURPRISE."

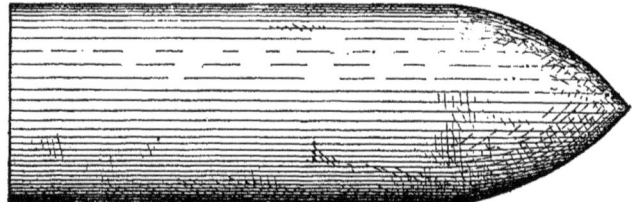

DR. J. H. McLEAN'S BOMB SHELL "SURPRISE."

This time shell, like the "Cyclone" is furnished with the time-firing mechanism, to be set so as to fire in one second, or in twenty-four hours, or longer, if required, after leaving the gun, and it, like the other, gives no external evidence of being a shell at all.

The claims for superiority which Dr. J. H. McLean urges for this shell, *over all others of like calibre,* are,

1st. It will never prematurely explode in the gun or near it.

2d. It will explode exactly at the time desired without fail.

3d. It possesses no burning fuse to give warning of its approach, or a clue to its character.

4th. It will not be suspected by the enemy of being a shell until it is forever too late to profit by the knowledge of its character.

5th. From the fact that its character cannot be known until it explodes, it may be thrown into a fort in large numbers, and set to burst in six hours; would be totally unsuspected by the garrison until too late to remedy the fatally misplaced confidence.

LET THIS POINT BE CAREFULLY EXAMINED.

From his batteries on Morris Island, Gen. Gillmore, in 1863, pitched 5,000 shells into Fort Wagner, principally six-inch. During the shelling the Confederates in Fort Wagner were securely housed in their bomb-proofs, and when the shelling ceased, they would sally forth and resume their posts of duty.

They felt perfectly secure.

They knew that all of the shells that were to burst had bursted, and that there could be no danger until shelling should be resumed from Morris's Island. Therefore the casualties were few.

But suppose, instead of the old fuse shell, 5,000 of Dr. J. H. McLean's "Surprise" shells had been thrown into that fort, set to burst in three hours, or part in one hour, part in two hours, part in three hours, and so on in intervals all through a day or a night.

What could the poor fellows in that fort do?

They could not remain forever crouched in their bomb-proofs.

Yet to venture forth would be to meet death from unknown sources at unknowable moments, and the results must inevitably be

PANIC AND EVACUATION!

because there could be no rest for the troops inside the fort.

They must first hide away from the incoming shells, and continue to hide away for many hours afterward, while these unmanageable and exasperatingly deliberate missiles were getting ready to burst.

And as soon as one installment finished bursting, another would be rained in, thus depriving the attacked from all opportunity of rest or evolution except under deadly peril.

In fact, there is not a situation in which time-shells are at all desirable, where the "Surprise" would not demonstrate its great superiority over anything now in use. It will not cost more than $1 more than a fuse-shell, and is $6 to $8 cheaper, because every one will do its duty just as required, and not more than one in three or four of the fuse-shells really do this.

These shells can be made from three inches in diameter up to any size required, and answer all the ordinary purposes of solid shot fired from rifled guns first, and would be regarded as such by the enemy until the contrary was cruelly learned.

Dr. J. H. McLEAN'S ROCKET SHRAPNEL SHELL.

The following illustration exhibits one of the most admirable shells for destroying earthworks, stampeding cavalry, or general use against a battle line ever invented:

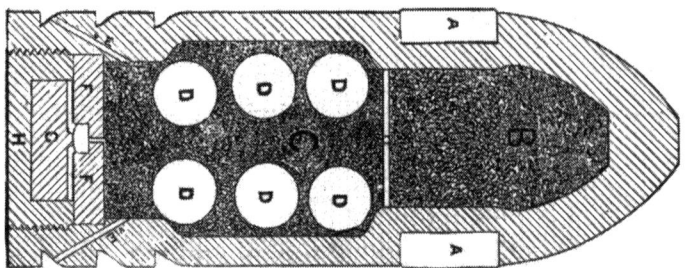

Dr. J. H. McLean's Rocket Shrapnel Shell.

A—Lead band.
B—Bursting charge.
C—Rocket powder.
D—Shrapnel shot.
E—Vents for the escape of the rocket powder.
F—Metal cap carrying primer.
G—Anvil for exploding the primer.
H—Metal head screwed into the shell.

The drawing pretty well explains itself, yet to make the direful character of this shell more clearly apparent, the reader's attention is directed to the fact, that when the shell is intended to destroy earthworks, it would be driven into such earthworks at a high velocity, say 2,000 feet per second, and upon striking the bank the rocket powder would be exploded by the percussion cap on the hammer, F, as it was forced against the anvil, G, by the concussion. As the rocket-powder escaped from the vents, E, the tendency would be to bury the shell deeper into the earth, and to finally tear a large gap in it, when the exploding charge, B, was reached.

When firing at cavalry, or at a battle-line, the velocity of the shell should be low, and it should strike the ground in front of the rank assailed, and ricochet to the mark. Upon touching the ground the rocket-powder would be ignited, and as it issues in fiery streams from the flying missile, horses would take fright and become unmanageable, and finally the shell would burst with a terrific detonation, and its fragments and the shrapnel it contained would create the usual havoc.

FOR SHELLING DISTANT CAMPS.

This missile will be found exceedingly effective, for if thrown from the gun at a high velocity and proper angle, it will be carried as far as any other projectile of like weight; then, upon touching the earth, the rocket-powder contained in it will be ignited, and a new impulse be given to its flight.

That these will be found to be a most serviceable and effective shell, there cannot be the smallest question.

Dr. J. H. McLEAN'S PERCUSSION SHELL.

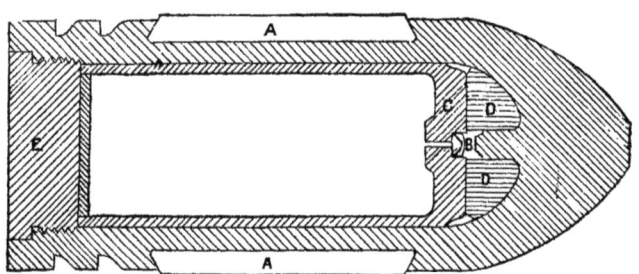

Dr. J. H. McLean's Percussion Shell.

A—Band of lead.
B—Anvil for exploding the primer.
C—Metal tube containing the bursting charge and primer.
D—Rubber cushions to prevent accidental discharge of shell.
E—Metal plug screwed in to close the shell.

There are situations where percussion shells are very serviceable; so much so that really good ones may be deemed well nigh indispensable. Admitting this to be so, Dr. J. H. McLean caused a thorough investigation to be made into existing percussion shells, to discover, if possible, their principal defects, and whether these defects could be remedied. The result has enabled Dr. McLean to present to the world a

PERCUSSION SHELL PERFECT IN EVERY PARTICULAR.

The defects in existing percussion shells are as follows:

1st. Uncertainty in exploding.

2d. Liability to explode if dropped while handling.

3d. Liability to explode when ricochetting on the water.

Dr. McLean claims to have successfully overcome all these objections in the percussion shell which he now presents to the belligerent world.

This shell is provided with the usual percussion primer, hammer and anvil, but the tube upon which the primer rests is imbedded so deep in a soft rubber cushion that neither the dropping of the shell nor its ricochetting upon the water will fire it. If it strikes the earth at any angle when fired from a gun, it will burst; therefore in using it against a battle-line, it should be made to strike the ground directly in front of the line, when it would instantly burst, and all of its particles be pitched violently forward into the line.

In shelling cavalry no such need exists, because, if the shell strike either horse or man, it would explode and scatter its fragments right and left, and beyond, with deadly effect.

THE WHOLE GROUND COVERED.

It will be seen at a glance that Dr. J. H. McLean has as carefully, thoroughly, and conscientiously covered the whole question of bomb shells and their defects, and been as successful in remedying them as he has in any of the other wonderful Peace-Makers presented to the world in this volume, and he agrees to give a good and substantial bond to any government who may decide to experiment with these shells, that if they are built as Dr. McLean directs, they will do all and more than is herein claimed for them, and that they will not cost more than other shells, and will accomplish thirty per cent. more than the best now in use.

INDEX.

	PAGE
A Battery of the Cannon of To-day in Action, Illustrated	126
Aerial Rocket Torpedoes, Description of	185
Aerial Rocket Torpedo, Illustration	186
American Brass Primer	115
"Annihilator," Description of	135
"Annihilator" Magazine Cannon, Illustration	136–137
Armor, Iron, Illustration of	26
Arms and Army of the Future, Illustration	166
Arms and Army of To-day, Illustration	165
Armstrong Guns	83
Art of War	23
Battle, a Line of, using Dr. McLean Arms and Iron Forms, Illustration	163
Battery Gun "Besom," Illustration	144
Battery of Dr. McLean's Magazine Cannon in Action, Illustration	128
Battery Guns	142
Battery Guns, Magazine, The "Lady McLean," Illustration	149–151
Battery Guns, Magazine, The "Pulverizer."	146
Bennett, Jas. Gordon, Magazine Rifle, Illustration	157
"Besom," Battery Gun, Illustration	144
"Besom," Description of	145
Blakeley Guns	83
Blockades Destroyed at Night, with "Octopus" or "Devil Fish" Torpedoes	177
"Bogardus" Magazine Shot Gun, Illustration	169
Bomb Shells	189
Brass Primer, American	115
Breastworks, Iron Forms, Illustration of	47–49
Bullet-proof Shelter, Illustration of	47
Bullet-proof Tent	41
Bursting of Cannon	101
Caisson, Illustration of	148
Cannon, a Perfect, according to some Writers	81
Cannon, Bursting of	101
Cannon, Defects in, by Gen. Gillmore	104
Cannon, Magazine, Description of	130
Cannon, Magazine	124
Cannon, Magazine, a Battery of, Galloping along a Line of Battle, Illustration	131
Cannon Magazine "Gen. Grant," Illustration	132–133
Cannon of To-day, a Battery of, in Action, Illustration	126
Chamber, Elastic	113
Coasts and Harbors of the U. S., Defenseless Condition of, by Hon. S. S. Cox	75
Coloney, Myron, Biography of	19
Coloney, Myron, Portrait	18
Constructing celebrated Guns, Methods of	92
Construction of "Hercules" Gun	93–116
Cox, Hon. S. S., Condition of U. S. Coast and Harbors	75
Customer, an Ugly, Illustration	170
"Cyclone," Incendiary Time Shell	190
Dahlgren Guns	83
Dangerous Trio, Illustration	168
Dedication	5
Defects in Cannon, by Gen. Gillmore	104
Defect in Trunnions	109
Defect of Recoil	106
Defects of Vent	114
Defenses, Seacoast, Gen. Gillmore on	67

	PAGE
Description of "Hercules" Gun	100
Destroying Blockades at Night with "Octopus" or "Devil Fish" Torpedoes, Illustration	177
"Devil Fish" or "Octopus" Torpedo, single, Illustration	179
"Devil Fish" Torpedo, Illustration	175
Elastic Chamber	113
English Quill Primer	115
Firing Mechanism of Torpedo, Description and Illustration	178
Floating Fortress, Description of	31
Floating Fortress, Sectional View	33–34
Forms, Iron	39
Fortress, Floating, Description of	31
Fortress, Floating, Sectional View	33–34
Fortress, Impregnable	26
Fortress, Impregnable Iron, Cleared for Action	29
Fortress, Impregnable Iron, in Time of Peace	28
Fortress, Impregnable Iron, Sectional View	30
Fort made of Iron Forms, Illustration of	51–54
"Gen. Grant," Magazine Cannon, Illustration	132–133
Gillmore (Gen.) on Defects in Cannon	104
Gillmore (Gen.) on Forts	24
Gillmore (Gen.) on Seacoast Defenses	67
Grand Tower Block, Dr. James H. McLean's, Illustration	16
Guns, Average Life of	85
Guns, Armstrong	84
Guns, Battery	142
Guns, Battery, "Besom," Illustration	144
Guns, Blakeley	83
Guns Burst, Why	84
Guns, Dahlgren	83
Gun, "Hercules," Construction of	93–116
Gun, "Hercules," Description of	100
Guns, "Hercules," Mounted in an Earthwork, Illustration	117
Gun, "Hercules," Sectional Views of	94
Guns, Krupp	84
Guns, Magazine Battery, the "Lady McLean," Illustration	149–151
Guns, Methods of Constructing celebrated	92
Guns, Parrot	83
Guns, Rodman	84
Guns, What is Known About	81
Guns, Woolwich, Life of	86
Guns, Whitworth	83
"Hercules" Gun, Construction of	93–116
"Hercules" Gun, Description of	100
"Hercules" Guns Mounted in an Earthwork, Illustration	117
"Hercules" Gun on Swift Iron Steamer, Illustration of	64
"Hercules" Gun, Sectional Views of	94
Hinged Iron Forms	39
Howitzer for Throwing Torpedoes, Illustration of	187
Hunter's Last Shot, Not the, Illustration	161
Hydrophone	80
Impregnable Iron Fortress, Sectional View	30
Impregnable Fortress	26
Impregnable Iron Fortress in Time of Peace	28

INDEX.

Entry	PAGE
Impregnable Iron Fortress Cleared for Action	29
Incendiary Time Shell "Cyclone," Description and Illustration	190
Inelastic Chamber	111
Introduction	7
Iron Armor, Illustration of	26
Iron Forms	39
Iron Forms in Battle Line, Illustration	163
Iron Forms for Breastworks, Illustration of	47–49
Iron Forms for a Fort, Illustration of	51–54
Iron Steamer with "Hercules" Gun, Illustration of	64
Iron War Ship, Description of	59
Iron War Ship, Illustration of	62
Krupp Guns	84
Laboratory, Dr. Jas. H. McLean's, Illustration	14
"Lady McLean," The, Magazine Battery Gun, Description of	150
"Lady McLean," The, Magazine Battery Gun, Illustration	149–151
"Lady McLean," The, Magazine Battery Gun going into action, Illustration	154
"Lady McLean," The, Magazine Battery Gun, Light Brigade charging, Illustration	153
Last shot, Not the Hunter's	161
Line of battle, using Dr. McLean Arms and Iron Forms, Illustration	163
Magazine Battery Guns, The "Lady McLean," Illustration	149–151
Magazine Battery Gun, The "Pulverizer," Illustration	146
Magazine Cannon	124
Magazine Cannon "Annihilator," Illustration	136–137
Magazine Cannon "Vixen," Illustration	139
Magazine Cannon "Gen. Grant," Illustration	132–133
Magazine Cannon, Description of	130
Magazine Cannon, Dr. McLean's, A battery of, in action, Illustration	128
Magazine Cannon, Battery of, galloping along a line of battle, Illustration	131
Magazine Gun, What constitutes a, Illustration	156
Magazine Pistol	167
Magazine Rifle, 64-Shot	158
Magazine Rifle, 32-Shot	158
Magazine Rifle "James Gordon Bennett," Illustration	157
Magazine Rifle 128-Shot	157
Magazine Small Arms	156
Magazine Shot Gun "Bogardus," Illustration	169
Methods of Constructing Celebrated Guns	92
Method of Preventing Recoil, Illustration	107
McLean, Dr. James H., Biography	11
McLean's, Dr. James H., Grand Tower Block, Illustration	16
McLean's, Dr. James H., Office and Laboratory. Illustration	14
McLean, Dr. Jas. H., Portrait, Frontispiece	
"Octopus" or "Devil Fish" Torpedo, Illustration	175
"Octopus" or "Devil Fish" Torpedo, single, Illustration	179
Parrot Guns	83
Percussion Shells, Illustration and Description	196
Perfect Cannon, according to some writers	81
Pistol, Magazine	167
Primers	115
Projectile Torpedo "Thunderbolt," Illustration	179
"Pulverizer," The, Description of	148
"Pulverizer," The, in action	147
"Pulverizer," The Magazine Battery Gun, Illustration	146
Quill Primer, English	115
Recoil, Defect of	106
Recoil, Method of Preventing, Illustration	107
Redan after its evacuation by the Russians, Illustration	55
Rifle, Magazine, 32-Shot	158
Rifle, Magazine, 64-Shot	158
Rifle, Magazine, 128-Shot	157
Rifle, Magazine, "James Gordon Bennett," Illustration	157
Rocket, Shrapnel Shell, Description	194
Rocket, Shrapnel Shell, Illustration	195
Rocket, Submarine Torpedo blowing up ship	185
Rocket, Submarine Torpedoes, Description	181
Rocket Torpedo, Aerial, Illustration of	186
Rocket Torpedoes, Aerial, Description of	185
Rocket Torpedo, Submarine, Illustration of	182–183
Rodman Guns	84
Shrapnel Shell, Rocket	195
Shrapnel Shell, Rocket, Description	194
Seacoast Defenses, Gen. Gillmore on	67
Shell, Percussion, Illustration and Description	196
Shell, Rocket Shrapnel, Description	194
Shell, Rocket Shrapnel, Illustration	195
Shelter, Bullet-proof, Illustration of	47
Ship, Improved Iron War, Description of	59
Ship, Improved Iron War, Illustration of	62
Shot Gun, Magazine, "Bogardus," Illustration	169
Small Arms, Magazine	156
Submarine Rocket Torpedoes, Description of	181
Submarine Rocket Torpedo, approaching ship, Illustration	184
"Surprise," Time Shell, Illustration and Description	192
Tent, Bullet-proof	41
Time Shell "Surprise," Illustration and Description	192
Time Shell "Cyclone," Incendiary, Illustration and Description	190
Torpedoes	172
Torpedoes, Aerial Rocket, Description of	185
Torpedo, Aerial Rocket, Illustration of	186
Torpedo Firing, Mechanism of, Illustration and Description	178
Torpedoes of the Future	174
Torpedo, "Octopus" or "Devil Fish"	175
Torpedo, "Octopus" or "Devil Fish," single, Illustration	179
Torpedo Projectile "Thunderbolt," Illustration	179
Torpedoes, Submarine Rocket, Description	181
Torpedo, Submarine Rocket, Illustration of	182–183
Torpedo, Submarine Rocket, blowing up ship	185
Torpedo, Submarine Rocket, approaching ship, Illustration	184
Trio, A Dangerous, Illustration	168
"Thunderbolt," Projectile Torpedo, Illustration	179
Trunnions, Defect in	109
Ugly Customer, An, Illustration	170
Vent, Defects of	114
"Vixen," Magazine Cannon, Illustration	139
War, Art of	28
What is Known About Guns	81
Whitworth Guns	83
Why Guns Burst	84
Windage, Description of	108
Windage, Illustration of	109
Woolwich Guns, Life of	87

www.ingramcontent.com/pod-product-compliance
Ingram Content Group UK Ltd.
Pitfield, Milton Keynes, MK11 3LW, UK
UKHW050416240426
12048UKWH00021B/1544